10 95

Explorer
with Kids

Barbara Bannister
and
Jan Carlile

ExplOregon with Kids

Copyright © by Barbara Bannister
and
Jan B. Carlile

ISBN: 0-939116-41-3

Library of Congress Catalog Number: 96-083175

Published by Frontier Publishing
1427-A S.E. 122nd A
Portland, OR 97233-1204

For order fulfillment contact your distributors and wholesalers, or   Jan B. Carlile
1011 Oakwood Circle
McMinnville, OR 97128
503-472-7061

Photos: Front Cover - Fogarty Beach State Park. Back Cover - (upper left - clockwise) High Desert Museum, Beach at Pacific City, Petting Zoo - Wildlife Safari, Mt. Bachelor, Wooden Shoe Tulip Fields, Canby

Printed in the United States of America

Foreword

Oregon has beautiful cities, sandy beaches, snow-capped mountains, steep canyons, lush valleys, majestic trees, and interesting deserts. Cascading waterfalls, meandering rivers, placid lakes, volcanic terrain, fossil beds, and the deep blue of the Pacific Ocean add to Oregon's diverse attractions. In short, Oregon has something for everyone! And that includes kids!

In this book we have tried to find and explore places in Oregon that kids will enjoy and that you will enjoy with them. The "hands-on activities" in many of the museums and Interpretive centers will help them develop a sense of history. The opportunities for hiking, swimming, climbing, skiing, and fishing are plentiful and sure to be enjoyed. Amusement parks, aquariums, and zoos are also listed attractions.

Since Oregon has more parks, beaches and other places of interest than we could list, we chose only the ones of special interest to kids. Our purpose is to help you find places to take kids that will be entertaining, educational, or both.

To help you know basic things about each place listed, we have used a key to help you quickly decide if the place is one you might be interested in. The key is always located directly under the location. See below for the explanation of symbols used.

You will find this book will contribute to your fun as you and your children Expl*Oregon.*

KEY:

Price: ✪ : free or small donation
$: cheap $$: moderate $$$: Expensive

RR: restrooms, PT: picnic tables, DW: drinking water,
I: information, R: restaurant, SB: snack bar or vending machines, GS: gift shop

Dedication

With love to the kids who made the trips of yesterday so much fun: Dan, Bob, Lori, and Eden, and to the kids of today: Jeff, Erin,Jeremy, Dustin, Nikki, Craig, Samantha, Andrea, and Sarah.

BB

Love to Levi, Ben, Carrie, and Paul for the inspiration and incentive to expl-Oregon as we traveled and camped in this beautiful state in years past....and to the new generation, Maya and Asa, who are giving us reason to explore some more!

JC

Table of Contents

Chapter One
Explore the Oregon Coast *1*

Chapter Two
Explore the Willamette Valley *37*

Chapter Three
*Explore the Portland,
Columbia Gorge, and Mt. Hood
Areas* *51*

Chapter Four
Explore Central Oregon *75*

Chapter Five
Explore Eastern Oregon *93*

Chapter Six
Explore Southern Oregon *103*

Index *117*

Chapter 1

Explore The Oregon Coast

Cities, Beaches and other Fun Places

1

Introduction

Oregon is one of the few states where the entire coast line belongs to the public. If you can find access to the beach, you are welcome to use it. Private property extends only to where the vegetation ends. Because of this, you will find that Oregon's beaches are very clean and seldom crowded. You can walk in any direction for as long as you like or until cliffs stop you.

The natural wonders of tide pools, crashing waves over rocks, the wooded foothills of the coast range, and long sandy beaches are awesome. But when you or the kids tire of natural beauty you can enjoy various museums, aquariums, special playgrounds, dune buggy riding, cheese factories, a wild animal petting zoo, and many other attractions.

The ocean waters are cold at most of the beaches, but this usually doesn't prevent children from wanting to venture in. Many places have undertows, so be sure to read the cautions which are posted in most areas. Because of these undertows it is always recommended to go in the water when the tide is coming in. Since the beaches are free and extend for the entire state, there are no life guards. During winter months the ocean storms are awe-inspiring but dangerous. At this time, be cautious of sneaker waves, and stay off the logs on the beach because they might roll and be extremely dangerous.

There are numerous campgrounds and state parks available on the Oregon Coast. There are also motels and resorts at many different price ranges. Whether you are planning a day trip or a longer stay, you may wish to try some of the many places listed here. We have listed the ones which we felt were most appealing to kids.

Spend some time at the coast and enjoy the beautiful Oregon beaches which are delightful at any time of year!

Pictures on page 1, clockwise from upper left: Cape Kiwanda - near Pacific City, Bandon, Oregon, Sand dunes on the Central Beaches, "D" River Wayside - Lincoln City, Center : Tide Pools - Central Oregon Beaches

The Northern Beaches

Astoria Area

ASTORIA COLUMN

Kids will enjoy the challenge of the 164 step climb to the top of the Astoria Column. Once at the top, from the viewing platform, they will be able to see a fantastic view of Astoria, the Columbia River , the nearby mountains, and the Pacific Ocean. A view of the Astoria Bridge, the longest continuous truss span bridge in the world, is also possible. The steps to climb to the top are inside the column, but outside, the newly refinished column is unique and provides a great history lesson. The friezes painted on the 125 foot column depict the early history of the Northwest. The fourteen scenes are painted in chronological order, starting at the base of the column. Some of the scenes depicted are of the time before the white men, the arrival of Lewis and Clark, the war between Great Britain and the United States in this area, and the development of the region. The column was built in 1926 to commemorate the discovery and settlement of the area. It was modeled after Trajan's Column in Rome, Italy. Open daily from 8 - to dusk.

Location: On Coxcomb Hill on the outskirts of Astoria. Watch for signs
✪, RR, DW, SB, GS

COLUMBIA MARITIME MUSEUM

This wonderful museum is the only accredited marine museum on the West Coast. Explore marine transportation from dugout canoes through the present. Many exhibits tell of the Columbia River and the Northwest Coast. Exhibits include artifacts, ship models, and photographs of the history of fishing, whaling, and marine transportation. The kids will enjoy boarding the Columbia River lightship which once guided ship pilots at the mouth of the Columbia. They can also walk the bridge of a World War II warship, or take a look at passing ships through a submarine periscope. Open daily from 9:30 to 5.

Location: 17th Street and Marine Drive, Astoria (503) 325-2323

$$, RR, DW, GS

FORT CLATSOP

Kids will enjoy seeing and walking through the replica of the fort built and used by Lewis and Clark during the winter of 1805-06. During the summer there are usually demonstrations by forest rangers of such things as candle-making, shooting muzzle- loaded flintlocks, moccasin making, and hollowing out of a canoe. There is a Junior Ranger Program in which children can participate in these or other activities and earn a certificate. The newly redone and expanded interpretive center in the park offers many opportunities to learn more about the exploration by Lewis and Clark. Children  can push a button to see and hear specific topics. There is a 32 minute film and a seventeen minute slide show which you may see if you wish. The grounds surrounding the interpretive center are beautiful. Open daily. Closed Christmas.

Location: Just off Highway 101, 6 miles west of Astoria (503) 861-2471

$ (Free from October - to March 1), RR, DW, PT, I, GS,

FORT STEVENS

Fort Stevens is a great place to spend the day or several days!

The fort was named for a Union General who was killed in the Civil War. It dates from that era. The fort was used  to guard the entrance to the Columbia River. During World War II, there was a gun battery at the fort. Japanese submarines shelled the area. This was the only place fired upon in the continental United States. This gun battery is abandoned and older kids will enjoy seeing it, climbing around in it, and reading about it. A museum within the park contains exhibits and you may also pick up a map for a self-guided walking tour. If you have bikes with you, there are seven miles of bike trails. Kid can run and play on the beach where the remains of Oregon's most famous shipwreck, the Peter Iredale, can still be seen. Let the kids try to capture the wreck on film. There are two sandy-beach swimming areas at Coffenbury Lake which is located in the park. Open daily.

Location: 10 miles west of Astoria off Highway 101. (503) 861-1671

$, RR, DW, PT, I, G

UPPERTOWN FIRE FIGHTERS MUSEUM

This former 1890's fire station will be of interest to kids of most ages. It houses a rare horse-drawn fire engine built in 1878. There is a 1912 fire truck which was America's first motorized fire engine. There are also examples of fire fighting equipment, illustrating how fire fighting has changed through the years. There will be a guide to tell you about the museum. Be sure to ask to hear the legend of the ghost of this museum. Sometimes children are allowed to sound an alarm or ring the engine bells. Open Friday - Sunday from 10:00 a.m. to 5 p.m. from May to September. Remainder of the year Friday - Sunday 11-4. Closed Thanksgiving, New Year's Day, and Christmas.

Location: 30th and Marine Drive, Astoria
$$, RR, PT, GS

Seaside Area

BUMPER CARS AND ARCADE

On the street in downtown Seaside, can be found two places where kids can let off some steam on days when the weather is not the best for outdoor activities. The bumper cars provide fun for all ages and nearby is an arcade featuring skee ball, shooting galleries, and video games.

Location: On Broadway in downtown Seaside
$$

CHILDREN'S NATURE MUSEUM

This hands-on children's museum, features hundreds of living animals. Reptiles, birds, mammals, and insects are among the exhibits. Animal skulls and skeletons will be of interest to kids. Minerals and fossils are also on display. Open daily from 10 A.M. to 7 P.M.

Location: 203 South Holladay Drive, Seaside (503) 738-4146
$$, RR, GS

THE SALT WORKS

The site where the Lewis and Clark expedition boiled sea water to obtain much-needed salt, is located in Seaside. The salt was obtained by boiling sea water in five large kettles. Even though the kettles boiled the water night and day, only three quarts of salt per day were produced. It took seven weeks for the men to obtain the four bushels of salt needed to preserve their food for the trip home. These salt works of Lewis and Clark have been reproduced from information found in the Lewis and Clark diaries. This is a quick but interesting stop for kids and adults alike.

Location: On Lewis and Clark Way, 8 blocks south of Broadway, between Beach Drive and the promenade.

❂, I

SAND BIKING

If you or the kids want to do more than run on the beach or build sand castles, you may wish to rent a sand bike, a moped, or an old-fashioned bicycle surrey. These may be rented at various places in downtown Seaside. Some of the rental places are: Distinctive Fun for All, (503)738-8447, Log, Inc. (503) 738-7663, and Manzanita Fun Cycles (503) 738-3703.

Location: Downtown Seaside
$$

SEASIDE AQUARIUM

This aquarium is fun for kids because they can feed the seals and feel various marine life in the touch tanks. The trained seals at the aquarium are amusing as they perform tricks for food or applause. The underground tanks contain many varieties of bright-colored sea life. A wolf eel, sand shark, and many types of crab are just a few of the many sea creatures on display. The Seaside aquarium is one of the oldest on the west coast. Open daily at 9 o'clock from March to October and Wednesday - Sunday from November through February.

Location: 200 N. Promenade, Seaside (503) 738-6211
$$, (Seaside Public Restrooms nearby), GS

TOWN CENTER CAROUSEL

Seaside is one of the oldest resort towns in Oregon and its carousel has long been a great attraction for visiting children. The old carousel was replaced in 1990 with an imaginative new ride that features such animals as a flying pig and a giant rabbit, as well twelve beautiful horses. Let the kids enjoy the ride and don't forget to take their picture.

Location: Seaside Town Center, 300 Broadway, (503) 738-6728
$

Tillamook Area

BLUE HERON CHEESE FACTORY

A free petting zoo including a burro, an Angora goat, nubian goats, a pygmy goat, chickens, and a cat is a highlight for young kids at this stop. Inside this converted Dutch dairy barn, there are free samples of various cheeses, spreads, jams, mustards, syrups, etc. An excellent gift shop and deli are also available Open daily.

Location: 2001 Blue Heron Drive, Tillamook (off Highway 101 (503) 842-8281
✪, RR, PT, R,

CAPE MEARES LIGHTHOUSE

Located in Cape Meares State Park is an interesting lighthouse. Visitors can walk up the circular stairway inside the lighthouse and see the inner workings of the light which was first illuminated in 1890. The state park which surrounds it contains the "Octopus Tree," a very large Sitka Spruce with a diameter of ten feet at the base. Other trails in the park lead to viewpoints overlooking areas inhabited by Steller sea lions and nesting sea birds.

Location: 10 miles south of Tillamook on The Three Capes Scenic Loop.
$, RR, PT, DW

LATIMER QUILT CENTER

Enjoy watching demonstrations of weaving, quilting, preparation of wool, tatting, and paper making. Some of the demonstrations allow hands-on participation. Classes in all of these arts are also available. Exhibits of these crafts are abundant and are changed several times a year. You may wish to walk through the adjacent dye garden on the center grounds. The center, itself, is located in an old school house. Open daily during the summer months. Closed Mondays from October 1 - April 1 and also Thanksgiving and Christmas.

Location: On Wilson River Loop Road, Tillamook
$, RR, PT

TILLAMOOK CHEESE FACTORY

Self-guided tours of this factory, which produces the famous Tillamook cheese, will interest young and old. This spotless factory is a popular tourist stop. Free samples of the famous cheese are available and the kids will enjoy an ice cream cone which you can buy from the ice cream bar. A busy restaurant and gift shop are also a part of your visit to the Tillamook Cheese Factory. Open daily, 8:00 a.m - 8:00 p.m from June -August and 8 - 6 for the remainder of the year.

Location: 4175 Highway 101 North, Tillamook (503) 842-4481

O, RR, DW, R, GS

TILLAMOOK COUNTY PIONEER MUSEUM

This pioneer museum has many excellent exhibits, including Indian bead and basket work, pioneer memorabilia, and local and foreign wildlife. The three floors of exhibits also include dioramas, and replicas of a blacksmith shop, a pioneer parlor, a pioneer kitchen, and a firefighters' lookout. In the basement section there is a display of antique automobiles including a 1902 Holsman. There is also an antique sleigh.

The lifelike preserved animal exhibits will interest children. Outside, on the museum grounds, is a large steam engine, called a steam donkey, which was used in logging. Open daily during the summer. Closed on Mondays from October 1 - April 1, and on Thanksgiving and Christmas. Check for times. Discount tickets are available at the Tillamook Chamber of Commerce., 3795 Highway 101 N.

Location: 2nd and Pacific, Tillamook (503) 842-4553
$, RR

TILLAMOOK NAVAL AIR STATION MUSEUM

World War II planes, including planes from both U. S. and foreign countries, are housed in this blimp hangar. This former U. S. air base is the largest wooden building in the world. In World War II, blimps were used to spot enemy submarines. Two of these blimps may be seen in the museum. Restoration of old planes is ongoing in this hangar. You can also see a replica of a World War II radio room and a replica of a World War II hospital room. Open daily. Discount coupons are sometimes available at the Tillamook Chamber of Commerce.

Location: 6030 Hangar Road, Tillamook (off Highway 101, four miles south of Tillamook) (503) 842-1130.
$$, RR, SB, GS

Pacific City Area

CAPE KIWANDA

Cape Kiwanda, with its awe-inspiring Haystack Rock, is one of the few places on the Oregon coast where boats may be taken directly into the surf. At this cape, fishermen use small boats known as dories. Both kids and adults will enjoy the excitement of watching these colorful dories as they are launched into the ocean and then again when they make their quick dash back onto the beach. Sit on a log or climb the nearby sand hill and watch the fishermen skillfully maneuver these intriguing boats. The kids will also have fun climbing to the top of the sand hill and running or rolling back down. A celebration known as Dory Days is held the third weekend in July. During this time there are boat races, a fish fry, and other activities. When the tide is out, take the kids and explore the tide pools below the cliff. As at all beaches, great care needs to be taken, to be sure the kids know the dangers of rocks, waves, and tides.

Location: Three Capes Scenic Loop
✪, RR, R

CENTRAL BEACHES

Lincoln City Area

ROADS END STATE WAYSIDE

If you or your kids like hunting for agates or other beach treasures, this is usually a good beach for it. The beach is also great for flying kites, throwing Frisbees, or playing in the sand.

Location: Off Highway 101, 1 mile north of Lincoln City
✪, RR, PT, DW

REGATTA GROUNDS PARK

A stop at Regatta Grounds Park is sure to please the kids. Because the park is located a mile from the ocean, it is often less windy and sometimes more sunny than are the ocean beaches. The park borders Devil's Lake and the sandy beach on its shores is sure to tempt the kids into building a sand castle. When they feel like swimming, there is a shallow, roped-off area where they can splash or swim. There are no life guards, however. A nature trail winds through the park and you may wish to explore it with the kids. Probably the most fun for the younger set is the fabulous playground, called Sandcastle Park. This playground was designed by Robert Leathers using suggestions by local schoolchildren. While it includes the traditional slides and swings, it also has such unusual features as a wolf tunnel, a fish fort, a bouncy whale, a tugboat, and a rope pulley. Devil's Lake was once the site of many sailboat regattas and a boat launch is also part of this park. The park is open daily from 6 a. m. until 10 p.m.

Location: West Devil's Lake Road,turn east off Highway 101, Lincoln City
✪, RR,PT, DW, I

D RIVER STATE WAYSIDE

Kite flying is an art at the D River State Wayside. Launch your own kites or watch professionals fly their gigantic, colorful windsocks or kites. Marvel at the stunt kites doing gymnastics in the sky. See windsocks of up to one hundred feet. The kites are flown almost every day but there are also two kite festivals held here in the spring and fall.

Kids will also enjoy the long sandy beach and the little D River, the shortest in the world, which flows into the ocean here. Put a blanket on the sand and enjoy a picnic while you watch the show!

Location: Highway 101, Central Lincoln City
❂, RR

Depoe Bay Area

FOGARTY CREEK STATE PARK

Fogarty Creek Park offers the best of both worlds for picnickers. If you prefer your sandwiches without sand, eat at picnic tables on the east side of the park. If you don't mind a little sand with your lunch, go under Highway 101 on a paved path, spread a blanket on the beach, and enjoy sights and sounds of the Pacific Ocean. Fogarty Creek divides the beach, and is a shallow delight to the kids. Large driftwood logs provide a backrest or a windbreak. A small fee is charged for each vehicle entering this day use park.

Location: 2 miles north of Depoe Bay
$, RR, PT, DW

DEPOE BAY

You can spend a fortune or get by for nothing when you visit lively Depoe Bay. Watch for whales from the sea wall for nothing or pay to go out on a whale watching boat for an exciting hour-long trip. You can stand at the bridge and enjoy watching the bright-colored fishing boats come and go, or you can pay to take a charter and go deep-sea fishing for yourself. Watch the waves crashing on the rocks from the observation deck of the Made-in-Oregon building on the ocean side of Highway 101, or for closer viewing, there are pay-telescopes on the top floor of the building. There are also public rest rooms in the basement. Be sure you do not allow the children to climb over the wall onto the rocks, for waves often sweep over these rocks and can be extremely dangerous. There are numerous other shops of all descriptions, snack bars, and restaurants in this busy tourist-town. A small aquarium is also located on the main street.

Location: South of Lincoln City on Highway 101
☉ (For whale or boat watching from the wall or bridge) $$$ (for charter boats), RR, DW, SB, R, GS

DEVIL'S PUNCH BOWL STATE PARK

When the kids gaze into the Devil's Punch Bowl, they will think it is awesome! The waters in the bowl come and go and bubble and spout, from the action of the winds, waves, and tides. At high tide the ocean roars into the bowl with a mighty splash. This bowl, which was once a cave, is marked by the many waves which have helped form it. Take time to pull off the highway and see the Devil's Punchbowl. Bring a picnic or enjoy a bowl of clam chowder at the nearby restaurant.

Location: 8 miles north of Newport, off Highway 101
☉, RR, PT, DW, R, GS

Newport Area

YAQUINA HEAD

It's worth a trip up the winding road that leads off of Highway 101 to Yaquina Head. While the main attraction will probably be the 1873 era lighthouse, there are many other things to interest you and the kids. The lighthouse is  open for tours from June to September. If you wish to see the tower watch room, plan to visit in the morning. In the afternoon only the lower rotunda is open. The kids will also enjoy standing on the wooden observation deck and spotting the seals and sea lions which may be frolicking in the water or sleeping on the large rocks visible below. They can also climb down to the newly developed beach tide pools which have paved walkways around them. In the summer there is often a forest ranger available to provide information or let you view the sea life through a telescope. Wild flowers are abundant during the summer and add to the beauty of Yaquina Head. An interpretive center is being built on one of the former quarries which are located off the road leading to the lighthouse. This center should be open in late 1996 or early 1997 Bring the camera so the kids can capture a great shot of the picturesque lighthouse or a view of the beautiful Pacific Ocean and its coastline.

Location: Off Highway 101, just north of Newport, (541) 265-2863

✪, RR,

U. S. COAST GUARD STATION

A tour of a working Coast Guard station might be fun and educational for you and the kids On the tour you can see films of the Coast Guard's history as well as seeing the men and women of the Coast Guard at work. You will also be able to board several of the boats of the Coast Guard This is a working station so call ahead for a reservation before your tour. Tours available from 8 - 12:30 and from 2:00 until 5.

Location: 541 SW Naterlin Drive, Newport (541) 265-5381
✪

YAQUINA BAY STATE PARK

The historical lighthouse in the park is fascinating to visit. It is not only a well-preserved lighthouse of the mid 1800's, but it also has a ghost story connected with it. The kids will enjoy hearing this ghostly tale and also learning about shipwrecks and the way of life for a lighthouse keeper. Sometimes children are invited to play a type of treasure hunt game during which they try to find various things as they tour the lighthouse. Some of the things they might be asked to locate are an old Bible, an inkwell, old kitchen utensils, an item of clothing, etc. Upon completion of the game, the children can receive a small prize from the gift shop downstairs. After your tour of the lighthouse, have a picnic in the park, or view whales or boats from the new observation deck. This is a day use only park. It is open daily, with the lighthouse open between noon and four during the summer. During the winter months the lighthouse is open only from Friday - Sunday.

Location: North of the Yaquina Bay Bridge, Newport
✪, RR, PT, DW, I, GS (in lighthouse)

HATFIELD MARINE SCIENCE CENTER

When the Hatfield Marine Science Center opens in September of 1996, it will certainly be worth a stop. The focus of the Center is on marine research and how it affects people. There will be permanent exhibits and changing ones. A favorite activity of children is a hands-on touching pool where kids can reach into the water and pick up an anemone or another sea creature. There is a tank with a live octopus which is interesting to see and hear about. Exhibits such as demonstrating how a satellite works in tracking whales will be interesting. In the summer this science center offers a guided 30-minute tour of Newport's docks or a longer estuary walk. Check for open times.

Location: 2030 S. Marine Science Drive, Newport (541) 867-0226
$$, RR, DW, I, GS

OREGON COAST AQUARIUM

This nationally acclaimed aquarium has many exhibits housed in natural habitat settings. Sea otters, a giant octopus, sea lions, puffins and other sea birds are housed in outdoor areas where you and the kids can walk at your own pace. There is also a huge new tank which was built for Keiko, the orca whale featured in the movie *Free Willie*. Kids will enjoy watching the antics of this large mammal. The natural settings with their sounds and sights add much to the aquarium Many exhibits can also be seen inside the aquarium, including both plant and animal life. The exhibits are divided into four different areas, all of which focus on the marine life of the coast. The feeding of the aquarium's animal life can be viewed by visitors. Special programs and demonstrations are often held.

Open daily, except Christmas. 9 - 6:00 March - October. 10 - 4:30 during the remainder of the year.

Location: 2820 S.E. Ferry Road, Off Highway 101, South of Yaquina Bay Bridge, Newport (541)867-3474
$$, RR , DW , I , R , GS

UNDERSEA GARDENS

Through large underwater windows, kids can view marine plants and animals in a natural habitat. Regular scuba diving shows are a feature of this aquarium. Open daily, except for Christmas. Summer 9-8, Remainder of the year 10-5.

Location: 250 S. W. Bay Blvd., Newport , (541) 265-2206

$$, RR,GS

The two following attractions share a common, restaurant, gift shop, and rest rooms.

RIPLEY'S BELIEVE IT OR NOT

Older kids will enjoy a visit to Ripley's Believe It Or Not. Oddities of all kinds will probably fascinate them. The kids can pretend they are astronauts speeding through space or meet Spock from Star Trek face-to-face. This sometimes scary (just what kids like) attraction is one they will remember. Open daily, except for Christmas. Summer 9-8, Remainder of the year 10-5.

Location: Mariner Square, 250 S.W. Bay Blvd. Newport, (541)265-2206

$$, RR, R, GS

THE WAX WORKS - A LIVING MUSEUM

Most kids will enjoy seeing wax figures, some animated, representing famous people or famous characters. The older kids will think it's great fun, but younger ones might be frightened unless you go with them. Let the older ones try to guess who the characters are. Open daily, except for Christmas. Summer 9-8, Remainder of the year 10-5.

Location: 250 S.W. Bay Blvd., Newport, (541)265-2206

$$, RR, R, GS

MIKE MILLER EDUCATIONAL AREA

This short, one-mile educational walking loop was designed with kids in mind. Visit old logging sites, railroads, and beaches. There are many interpretive signs along the trail You may want to see how many different kinds of wildlife you can spot as you hike the loop. Open daily.

Location: Off Highway 101, 2 miles south of Yaquina Bay Bridge

✪

Waldport - Yachats Area

HISTORIC ALSEA BAY BRIDGE INTERPRETIVE CENTER

Kids can build a bridge out of wood or from pipe in this new interpretive center. There are also interactive displays where they can guess how long it took to go from one end of the Oregon coast to the other in different eras. There are also video presentations depicting the history of the area and of the Alsea Bay Bridge. Open Tuesday - Saturday from 9:00 - 4:00.

Location: Directly south of Alsea Bay Bridge on Highway 101

✪, RR, PT, DW, I, GS

YACHATS COMMONS PLAYGROUND

Do the kids need to stretch their legs after being cooped up in the car? Pull off Highway 101 into the Yachats Commons Playground Behind the Commons building, there is a small playground that the young ones will enjoy. A tugboat is there to climb on as well as more usual equipment. A large grassy area for sitting or running is available. Sit on the grass and watch the kids get the kinks out!

Location: Highway 101 and 4th Street, Yachats

✪

CAPE PERPETUA VISITORS CENTER

This "kid-friendly" center, located east of Highway 101, is worth the trip up the winding road. Eleven treasure chests, filled with hands-on activities appealing to all ages, are a special feature. Some of the treasure chests include activities to do with whales, fossils, shells, and tide pools. A "create your own forest" activity is a feature of another chest. Many native American artifacts are in the center. A spectacular view is seen from the large picture window in this lovely center. Videos and films are also available for viewing. Outside there are 22 miles of hiking trails with a couple of two-mile round trip trails which kids could easily manage. Open daily 9-5 in the summer, Open weekends 10-4 during the winter months.

Location: East of Highway 101 between Heceta Head & Yachats, (541) 547-3289
❂, RR, PT, DW , I , GS

SOUTHERN OREGON BEACHES

Florence Area

DEVIL'S ELBOW STATE PARK

Get out of the car and stretch at Devil's Elbow State Park. Bring a picnic and enjoy a few hours in this beautiful park. You and the kids can run on the beach or hike on inland hiking trails. Bring the camera for great pictures of not only the kids, but also of the rock formations out in the water. In this cozy cove there is also a trail leading to Heceta Head Lighthouse to the north. This lighthouse is said to be one of the most photographed lighthouses in the world. Day-Use only park, open year round.

Location: 13 miles north of Florence on Highway 101
$, RR, PT, DW

SEA LION CAVES

The kids (and you) will probably be awed by some of the sights at Sea Lion Caves. These caves began forming 25 million years ago and now rise to a height of over 200 feet. The length of the main cavern is over 100 feet. Even though this has been developed as a tourist attraction, care is taken to preserve the natural habitat. Your self-guided tour begins at viewing platforms where you may use your own binoculars or the pay telescopes to see the sea lions, sea birds, and sometimes migrating whales in the water below. Then take an elevator to a depth of over 200 feet to the gigantic cave where the sea lions are found in abundance. At times, depending on the season, you might get to see sea lion mothers and their babies. The young sea lions are especially fun to watch as they learn to swim and play in the waves. When you ascend again to the outdoors, some of the interesting things to be seen, other than the birds and sea lions, are wild flowers and a spectacular view of Heceta Head Lighthouse. Plan at least an hour for your visit. Open all year Daily 9-dusk during July - August, 9-4 remainder of the year. Closed on Christmas

Location: 91560 Highway 101, 11 miles north of Florence, (541) 547-3111
$$, RR, DW, I, SB, GS

C & M STABLES

Even children and adults who are totally inexperienced around horses, might enjoy the fun of horseback riding on the beach. Patient horses and handlers accommodate every skill level. Beach rides, coast range rides, and corral rides are available from these stables. 1 1/2 or 2 hour sunset rides are offered and there are extra short trips for young children. Open all year.

Location: 8 miles north of Florence on Highway 101, (541) 997-7540
$$$, RR, PT, DW, SB

DARLINGTONIA WAYSIDE

Carnivorous plants are usually fascinating to kids, and the Darlingtonia Wayside has plenty of them! A raised boardwalk carries you past skunk cabbages to the Darlingtonia plants. These exotic cobra lilies lure insects to their doom. The bugs, who enter the mouth of the plant,enticed by its sweet smell, fall into the plant and are digested. The lilies bloom in May and June. Information on the lilies and their life cycle is plentiful. This wayside is small but an interesting one. If you think your children will be interested, make a quick stop to see these exotic plants. Day-Use only.

Location: 5 miles north of Florence on Highway 101
✪, RR, PT, DW, I

DOLLY WARES DOLL MUSEUM

If you have kids who like dolls, you may want to stop and visit this museum, containing 2500 dolls of all ages and descriptions. The collection includes dolls from many countries including France, Germany, and Italy. It also has a doll dating from pre-Columbian times. There are beautifully costumed dolls from the late 1800's and early 1900's, but there are also the more modern dolls which you and the kids may recognize. Some of the early modern dolls which collectors prize are sets of Dionne quintuplets, Effanbee's Patsy dolls, several Shirley Temple dolls, Kewpie dolls, and many others. Dolls made of china, bisque, wood, iron, felt, celluloid, plastic, and vinyl are all represented. Open daily from 10-5. Closed on Mondays.

Location: On U.S. 101 at 36th Street, Florence (541) 997-3391
$$, GS

SANDLAND ADVENTURES

Fun-lovers of all ages will enjoy a stop at Sandland Adventures. This attraction features dune buggy rides. You may rent a dune buggy or a four wheeler or let experienced drivers take you on a tour. Other attractions are: bumper boats, go carts, and miniature golf. Open daily 9-

7:30 from June 1 - Labor Day. Open 9-5 during the rest of the year. Closed January 1 and December 25th.

Location: Highway 101, 2 miles south of Florence, (541) 997-8087
$$$, RR, PT, DW, SB, GS

HONEYMAN STATE PARK

Take a hike or go swimming in beautiful Honeyman State Park. If you have a boat or canoe with you, you will find a boat launch available, or you can rent a canoe, row-boat, or paddle boat at the concession stand in the park. There is a roped-off area of shallow water for young water lovers. The paved path around the lake leads to the sand dunes and is user-friendly for strollers and young walkers. Kids of all ages will enjoy climbing on the dunes. If you are lucky enough to be there in the spring, you will be awe-struck by the beautiful, towering old rhododendrons which bloom at that time. Open year round.

Location: 3 miles south of Florence off Highway 101
$, RR, PT, DW, I, R

SAND DUNES FRONTIER AND THEME PARK

Whole families can enjoy a scenic tour of the sand dunes on open-air buses. Dune buggy rides are also available with experienced drivers. It is also possible to rent a ve-hicle for your own sand dune exploration. Only licensed drivers are allowed to do this. Other available activities are a nature trail, miniature golf, and a shooting gallery. Open daily from March 1 - November 1.

Location: 4 miles south of Florence on Highway 101 (541) 997-8087
$$$, RR, SB, GS

OREGON DUNES NATIONAL RECREATION AREA

Sand dunes, forests, lakes, and streams are all part of the Oregon Dunes National Recreation Area which extends along highway 101 from Florence to North Bend. Several access roads lead to the dunes. Along some of these roads, you may rent a dune buggy or other vehicle to explore the dunes, or you can take one of the hiking trails and hike through the area to the beach. You may camp in the area for a fee. Day use of the park is free. For more information, maps and videos about the area, stop at the Oregon Dunes National Recreation Area Headquarters at 855 Highway Avenue (Highway 101), Reedsport.

Location: Off Highway 101 from Florence to North Bend (541) 271-3611

✪, RR,

Reedsport Area

BOATING ON THE UMPQUA RIVER

If you would like a jet boat cruise of the Umpqua River, there are several different companies in the Reedsport area that offer these rides. Contact the Lower Umpqua Chamber of Commerce for information.

Location: 805 U.S. 101, Reedsport. 1-800-247-2155 or (541) 271-3495

$$$

UMPQUA DISCOVERY CENTER

Displays featuring tides, weather, bird eggs, or logging are featured in the Umpqua Discovery Center. The center is divided into two parts, one features the Antarctic and the other focuses on the coast. The Antarctic section features a large statue of Antarctic explorer Richard Byrd, and has examples of the primitive "snowmobiles" which were used in those early explorations. It also has a tent and clothing from the explorations. Exhibits may change from time to time The other section has a large working periscope and several "hands-on" exhibits. There are many videos and a large viewing room which can be used if you wish. The excellent gift shop features educational and science-oriented items relating to the coast and its wildlife. Open daily. May 15-Sept. 30 from 10-6, remainder of the year from 10 - 4.

Location: 409 Riverfront Way, Old Town Reedsport. (541) 271-4816
$, RR, PT (outside of center), DW, I, GS

THE HERO

The Hero, a wooden 1968 sailing vessel, is docked outside the Umpqua Discovery Center and tickets for a tour of the ship are purchased in the Center. The wooden ship, built for polar exploration and scientific research in the Antarctic, was retired in 1985 and was sailed to Reedsport to be converted into a floating museum. This 125 foot boat is equipped with two laboratories which were formerly used for biological, oceanographical, and geographical studies of the Antarctic. Open daily from 10-6, May 15 - Sept. 30th. Open 10-4 remainder of year. Check for tour times.

Location: Old Town Reedsport waterfront, (541) 271-4816
$$ (under five- free)

DEAN CREEK ELK VIEWING AREA

Morning and late afternoon are the best time to spot the elk herd that roams the 900 acres in this viewing area. There are many parking areas, but because the herd moves around they may or may not be in spotting distance of any particular place. Other wildlife which might be seen are ospreys, bald eagles, great blue herons, Canada geese, and many other smaller birds. Pull into one of the viewing areas and see how many different types of wildlife you can spot and identify. Bring your own binoculars or there are pay telescopes at some of the viewing stations. Open daily.

Location: Off Oregon 38, 3 miles east of Reedsport ✪, RR, DW, I

UMPQUA RIVER LIGHTHOUSE STATE PARK

A variety of things to do is a feature of this park. There are hiking trails, camping grounds, a lovely lake, an historic lighthouse, and a museum on the grounds. Lake Marie is especially attractive to kids because of the sandy beach and swimming opportunities. There is also a trail around the lake. The wooded areas around Lake Marie make it especially beautiful. You may watch whales from a platform across from the Umpqua Lighthouse. The still-working lighthouse is slated to be open to the public for tours on a regular basis from May to September. Check ahead for times. The small museum on the grounds tells about early life-saving equipment and services.

Location: 3 miles south of Reedsport off Highway 101 (541) 271-4631
$, RR, PT, DW

Northbend Area

COAST GUARD AIR STATION

The U.S. Coast Guard Station, located near the North Bend airport, is interesting because visitors can get a close look at the helicopters which fly out of the station. Since it is a working station, call to confirm the availability of a tour.

Location: Near the airport at North Bend, (541) 756-9214
✪

EMPIRE LAKES PARK

Paved hiking trails, a lakeside beach, fishing areas, and beautiful scenery are all features of this park. Stretch your legs and let the kids run at Empire Lakes Park.

Location: Follow signs to Charleston from Highway 101, off Newmark Avenue, North Bend
✪, RR, PT, DW

TENMILE LAKES COUNTY PARK

If you like to boat or fish, stop at the Tenmile Lakes County Park. This is the fourth largest lake in Oregon and its many arms make it an interesting one to explore. You can fish from the bank but for the best fishing, bring your own boat or rent one at the marina in Lakeside. A boat ramp is available for your motor boat or sailboat. For those who choose to do their fishing from the bank, there  is a popular fishing pier. There is also a fish cleaning station for all the fish you'll catch. You may be lucky and see an osprey or a bald eagle.

Location: Adjacent to the city of Lakeside
✪, RR, PT, DW

BASTENDORFF COUNTY PARK

Bastendorff County Park is a great place to spend a day or go camping. No reservations are required. The beach is seldom crowded and is great for long walks, Frisbee throwing, and kite flying. In an upper area above the beach there is play equipment which features a fort for kids to climb on and a wooden boat. There are horseshoe pits for older kids or adults and basketball courts. There are many picnic tables in convenient shelters and on the grass. A fantastic view is also a feature of the upper park.

Location: Turn right at county park off Cape Arago Highway

✪ (day use), $ (camping), RR, PT, DW

SUNSET BAY STATE PARK

For some of the warmest water on the coast, stop at Sunset Bay State Park. The sun often warms up the water in the cove to a temperature not found in most areas of the Oregon Coast. The incoming waves are blocked so the water is also calmer. This is a popular park so come early for the best picnic spots. Day use is in one area of the park and there is a camping area to the east.

Location: 3 miles southwest of Charleston on the Cape Arago Highway (541) 888-4902

$, RR, PT, DW

SHORE ACRES BOTANICAL GARDENS STATE PARK

To see beautiful gardens high above the surf, travel to Shore Acres Botanical Gardens State Park. Formal gardens are ablaze with flowers from spring to October. During the winter holidays the gardens are ablaze with over 150,000 lights. The gardens were once a part of the Louis Simpson estate. The story of Simpson, a lumber baron, and developer of North Bend, is told in the house located on the garden grounds. While walking in the gardens you and the kids may hear the barking of seals far below. If you wish to see them, travel a little farther south from

Shore Acres on the Cape Arago Highway and you will come to the Simpson Reef Overlook where you can look down below and see the seals in the water and on the rocks. Day use park. Open from dawn to dusk.

Location: Four miles southwest of Charleston on Cape Arago Highway 1-800-824-8486
$, RR, PT, I, GS

Coos Bay Area

MARSHFIELD SUN

For a glimpse of an old time newspaper office, take the kids to the Marshfield Sun. The vintage press is still operable and you can see cases of old type and newspapers from the past. Open on a regular basis during the summer months, Tuesday through Saturday from 1 to 4. In the winter it is open by appointment only.

Location: North 1st Street, Coos Bay 1-800-824-8486
✪

COOS BAY DOWNTOWN BOARDWALK

The whole family might enjoy seeing a working waterfront. You can watch the big ships head up the channel and see the tug boats at work. Coos Bay is an active port from which many large ships depart carrying wood chips, lumber, logs, or minerals. Take a walk on this attractive boardwalk for a close-up look at a busy port. Check with the Chamber of Commerce across the street for more information.

Location: Adjacent to Highway 101
✪

MENASHA TIMBER CORPORATION WOODS TOUR

Take the kids through a working forest on a guided tour led by a professional forester. Free transportation to the sight of the tour is provided from the Bay Area Chamber of Commerce, Coos Bay. Tours available from June - September. 1-800-234-1193

Location: Bay Area Chamber of Commerce, 50 East Central, Coos Bay. 1-800-824-8486
✪

COAST GUARD CUTTER ORCAS

This active Coast Guard Cutter is at sea 40% of the time, but if it is in port, visitors are welcome to a half hour tour. The entire top deck of this 110 foot ship is open for kids to explore. It is best to call ahead to make arrangements for your tour so that the crew can ready the ship by uncovering the 50-caliber machine guns and other armaments.

Location: On the waterfront at Coos Bay (541) 756-9214
✪

MINGUS PARK

Bring bread for the ducks that swim in the duck pond in Mingus Park. The pond has several fountains which spray the ducks and make the pond more attractive. A paved walk leads around the pond. There is also a great assortment of play equipment in two separate playgrounds. An 18-hole Frisbee golf course is popular with kids and adults. An outdoor swimming pool is open during the summer months. Another feature of this park, is a small Japanese garden, being developed with the help of the city of Choshi, Coos Bay's sister city in Japan.

Location: Downtown Coos Bay, Off Highway 101, west onto Commercial Turn right on 10th
✪ (fee for the swimming pool), RR, PT, DW

Bandon Area

WEST COAST GAME PARK SAFARI

Delight the kids with a stop at the West Coast Game Park Safari, the largest wild animal petting zoo in America. Take a picture of the kids petting, a cub, pup, or a kit and let them observe the many species of wild life living here. This park, which is dedicated to preserving wildlife, features over 450 creatures of 75 species. Some of these are: lions, tigers, bears, leopards, panthers, cougars, bison, lynx, zebras, camels, and elk. Many of the more tame animals mingle freely with the visitors. Open daily in the summer from 9:00 - 7:30. Open spring and Fall from 9 - 5. Open in January And February on weekends and holidays only.

Location: Highway 101, 7 miles south of Bandon. (541) 347-3106
$$, RR, DW, GS

BANDON CHEESE

Watch through picture windows as the famous Bandon cheese is made. The cheese is made on Tuesdays, Thursdays, and Saturdays. If you cannot come on one of these days, you still might like to stop at this small factory and have a free sample of the many different kinds of cheese available. The shop also features gigantic scoops of delicious ice cream. Be careful of the size you order for they are big!

Location: 680 East 2nd St., Bandon, (541) 347-2456
✪, I, SB, GS

Other Areas

JET BOATING

Take an exciting trip up the Rogue River in a speedy jet boat. Many different companies are available to take you on such a ride. The rides begin in Gold Beach and are of different prices and lengths. Some trips take time for lunch in Agness, and others are overnight excursions. Watch for wildlife on your trip and you may see deer, river otters, ospreys, and bald eagles.

Location: Gold Beach Chamber of Commerce, 1225 S. Ellensburg, 1-800-525-2334, (541)247-7526
$$$

PREHISTORIC GARDENS
Follow the dinosaur tracks in this kid-pleasing attraction which has been open since 1955. A coastal rain forest is the setting for these dinosaur replicas. The kids will enjoy having their picture taken beside a fierce life size dinosaur. The dinosaurs are created to scientifically correct size, shape, and details, based on the research of world-famous paleontologists. There are interpretive signs beside each dinosaur, telling about it and giving the correct pronunciation. There are also signs detailing the different types of plants, when they appeared on earth, and their characteristics. The chart detailing the rainfall in the gardens is also interesting. The trip through the gardens is a self-guided tour so you may take as much time as you wish. This is a cool stop on a hot day and one that most will enjoy. Open all year, daily from 8:00 a. m. until dusk.

Location: 36848 Highway 101 South, Port Orford (541) 332-4463
$$, RR, SB, GS

LOEB STATE PARK
If California is not on your agenda, stop at Loeb State Park and you can see redwoods without crossing the state line. There is a redwoods nature trail to explore. You can stay for a few hours or camp overnight.

Location: Off Highway 101, 10 miles northeast of Brookings.
$ (for camping), RR, PT, DW

Notes

Notes

Chapter 2

Explore The Willamette Valley

2

INTRODUCTION

The fertile Willamette Valley must have seemed like a paradise to the weary Oregon Trail Pioneers. Even today travelers are amazed at the beauty of this valley with its farmland, forests, foothills, and mighty rivers. The mild temperatures in both summer and winter also add appeal to the region. The plentiful rains in the winter months make the area green and productive, but the months of July, August, and September can usually be depended on to be warm and sunny.

Countless parks, waterfalls, lakes, beautiful trees, acres of flowers, and lush farmland, all against a backdrop of breathtaking Mt. Hood and Mt. Jefferson, make this valley very attractive. Its many covered bridges are picturesque and interesting.

Other attractions are the state capitol, children's museums, amusement parks, places of historical interest, and numerous opportunities for camping, swimming, hiking, fishing, and boating.

You will not have to travel far in any direction to find something of interest for you and your family in the beautiful Willamette Valley. We could not list all the many parks in the area. Corvallis, alone, has over thirty parks. Most of the parks have playground equipment, picnic areas, etc. so there are many to choose from. We listed the parks and other places which are of particular appeal to children. Choose the ones most suited to your kids and enjoy exploring this area with its diverse attractions and lovely scenery.

Pictures on preceding page, clockwise from upper left: Gilbert House Children's Museum - Salem, Enchanted Forest - near Salem, Flying M Ranch - near McMinnville, Center: Oregon State Capitol - Salem, Amazon Park - Eugene,

The Willamette Vallley

Eugene Area

AMAZON PARK

A playground with traditional and unusual play equipment is a feature of this park. A large wading pool for the younger set offers a cooling splash on a hot day. Older kids and adults may pay a small fee and use the larger pool, located nearby. This large, well-planned park is a great place to picnic, swim, and play.

Location: 26th and Hilyard, Eugene, OR
✪, RR, PT, DW

LANE COUNTY ICE

Take time out for a cool visit to Lane County Ice, one of only four indoor ice arenas in Oregon. Skates may be rented at the arena. Open daily for public skating. Call for times.

Location: 796 West 13th (at the fairgrounds), (541) 687-3615
$, RR, SB, GS

LOOKOUT CREEK OLD GROWTH TRAIL

If you'd like the kids to get a look at an old growth forest, a map for a trail through the pristine wilderness is now available at map outlets or from OLD GROWTH DAY HIKES, P. O Box 11288, Eugene, 97440. The trails are marked for difficulty and handicap accessibility. Old growth noble firs, Douglas firs, yellow cedar, red cedar, incense cedar, hemlock, and Ponderosa pines are visible from the trails. Some of the trees are as old as 800 years.

Location: Willamette National Forest
$$ (for map of trails)

MUSEUM OF NATURAL HISTORY

Changing exhibits of cultures around the world are a feature of this museum located on the campus of the University of Oregon. Exhibits relate to anthropology, archeology, and the natural sciences, especially relating to the Pacific Northwest. There may be a fee for special exhibits. Open Wednesday - Sunday from noon to 5:00.

Location: 1680 East 15th Avenue, Eugene. (541) 346-3024
✪, RR, DW

SARAGOSA OLD WEST RECREATION PARK

Experience a taste of Old Oregon history at Saragosa Old West Recreation Park. There are exhibits of pioneer life in an old west setting. There is a reconstruction of an old western village, including a jailhouse and a photographer's shop. Stage coach rides, special shows and events, and barnyard animals are also featured. Open May - October, W-F 10-6, Sat. - Sun. 8-6.

Location: 83263 Territorial Road, Eugene (541) 485-0038
$ (kids under 3 are free), RR, PT, DW, GS

SATURDAY MARKET

Every Saturday from April - November, a two-block area in downtown Eugene, hosts the Saturday Market. Live entertainment, an international food court, and countless booths featuring arts and crafts will amuse both adults and kids.

Location: 8th and Oak Street, downtown Eugene. (541) 686-8885
✪, RR, DW, SB, GS

SPLASH! THE LIVELY PARK SWIM CENTER

A wave pool, a lap pool, kiddie pool, and whirl pool are all available at this enjoyable swim center. Swish down the 136 foot water slide or experience four foot surf waves. Little ones in the family will enjoy the splashing in the kiddie pool, designed just for them.

Location: 6100 Thurston Rd., Springfield, (541) 747-9283
$$, RR, DW, SB

WISTEC CHILDREN'S MUSEUM

The Willamette Institute of Science & Technology Center (WISTEC) features hands-on science activities, traveling exhibitions, and special events. The changing exhibits make it a worth-while stop even if you've been there before. Young children learn as they play, doing such things as sorting, pouring things, working zippers, using crayons or paints, and using simple tools. Older kids can learn by using simple microscopes, thermometers, and scales. There are things to interest all ages. Open Wednesday - Sunday from noon until 6.

Location: 2300 Leo Harris Parkway, Eugene (541) 484-9027
$, RR, DW, GS

Salem Area

ENCHANTED FOREST

A world of fantasy, complete with storybook characters, awaits the visitors to the Enchanted Forest. A haunted house will thrill the kids, or they can explore Fort Fearless in the mining town of Toftville. An exciting ride on the ice mountain bobsled is sure to delight. A trip though the Old World Village will transport the kids back through time. Everyone will enjoy seeing the Fantasy Fountain dazzling water-light show. During the summer months, live entertainment at the Fairweather Theater is offered without additional charge. Picnic tables are available if you wish to bring your own lunch, or there are snack bars on the grounds There are ongoing changes and developments, so visitors may find more to see than they planned on. Open March 15 - September 30 from 9:30 - 6.

Location: 8462 Enchanted Way, S. E., Turner, OR (Off Interstate 5 - Exit 248) , (503) 363-3060
$$$, RR, PT, DW, SB, GS

SWEETBRIER PARK

Take a ride on the Bindlestiff and Brier Railroad in Sweetbrier Park. You may ride on the Audra K., a 2 foot gauge train, or board the Lucy B. Trolley. The ride takes fifteen minutes as it travels through scenic wild woods and an inspirational old-growth "Cathedral Grove." The price of the ride is included in the entrance fee and unless they are very busy, you may ride as often as you wish. You may also explore sites of petrified wood or old Indian camping grounds. Take a picnic and have lunch in picnic areas which are equipped with some cooking facilities. Volleyball and badminton courts are also available. There are hay bale castle forts for the little ones to climb on. In season you may also pick wild plums or blackberries. Open during the summer months from noon to 5 on Saturday, Sunday, and holidays. Reservations can also be made for special events such as birthdays, family reunions, etc.

Location: 43425 Highway 226, Scio (From Salem take Highway 22 & turn right at Hwy 226) (503) 859-2774
$, RR, PT, DW, GS

THRILLVILLE, USA

Next to the Enchanted Forest is an amusement park, Thrillville, USA. It features a large roller coaster, said to be the most thrilling in Oregon. Giant waterslides, bumper boats, Go-Karts, mini-golf, kiddie rides, classic rides, thrill rides, and games of skill are other features of the park. A picnic area is available. Check for hours.

Location: 8372 Enchanted Way, SE, Turner, OR (Off Interstate 5 - Exit 248), (503) 363-4095
$$$, RR, PT, DW, SB, GS

GILBERT HOUSE CHILDREN'S MUSEUM

The Gilbert House Children's Museum is a hands-on museum, housed in two Victorian homes. It is a member of the Association of Science & Technology Centers. Children of various ages can have fun blowing giant bubbles, having fun with arts and crafts, building things, using puppets, exploring science concepts and participating in various drop-in classes. A new exhibit is Recycle City which is completely hands-on and interactive. Children can have fun exploring Recycle City learning about problems of solid waste and how reduction, recycling, and reusing can help. The museum also has an Outdoor Science Center.

Location:116 Marion Street, N.E., Salem (503) 371-3631
$$ (2 and under free), RR, DW, GS

MISSION MILL VILLAGE

Take a walk-back in time by visiting the Mission Mill Village. The village is on a five-acre park. Included on the grounds are a textile museum, a museum store, Salem Visitor Center, historic homes, cafes, a mill stream, and gift shops. After a visit through the quaint village, enjoy a picnic lunch by the old mill stream. The kids will enjoy feeding the ducks that cluster near the

bridge. Food for the ducks is available from vending machines. Open daily 10:00 - 4:30 year round.

Location: 1313 Mill Street SE, Salem. 1-800-874-7012
$ (stores and grounds can be visited without a fee), RR, PT, R, I, GS

OREGON STATE CAPITOL BUILDING

A visit to any state is not complete without a stop at the state's capitol building. The shining golden pioneer on the top of this beautiful building can be seen for miles around. Oregon's capitol is of modern Greek design and features four different types of marble. Depression area art graces the interior. Large murals surround the rotunda and trace the history of Oregon. You might like to see if the kids can tell you what the murals depict. A large information center offering information about the entire state, is located in the lobby. Tour this lovely capitol on your own or join the tours which leave on the hour from Memorial Day through Labor Day. Open Monday - Friday, 7:30 a. m. - 5:00 p. m. Saturday, 9:00 - 4:00, Sunday, Noon to 4:00.

Location: 900 Court Street, N.E., Salem (503)986-1388
✪, RR, DW, R, I, GS

Other Areas

FLOWER GARDENS IN THE WILLAMETTE VALLEY

If you think that kids don't enjoy flower gardens, try them on some of the beautiful gardens in the Willamette Valley. The mild climate makes the valley a great place for propagating many types of flowers. The little ones love to skip down the rows of brightly colored tulips at the Wooden Shoe Tulip Beds. The more formally landscaped iris beds of Cooley's Iris gardens or Schreiner's Iris Gardens are also pleasing to kids. At Swan Island Dahlias the rows of vibrantly colored dahlias of all shades and sizes will make everyone from youngsters to seniors, want to take the perfect picture. The Flower Farmer near Swan Island Dahlias has a train which takes visitors around the acres of beautiful flowers. Most of the gardens have gift shops and the bulbs, rhizomes, and tubers can be purchased and they will be shipped to you at the proper time for planting. Maybe you'd like the kids to pick out 2 or 3 and let them try to grow their own beautiful flowers. The tulip beds are usually best for viewing from late April to early May, the iris gardens from middle May to early June, and the dahlia beds are brightest and most appealing from the middle of July until late September.

Location: The Flower Farmer: 2512 N. Holly, Canby (503) 266-3581

Cooley's Iris Gardens: 1153 Silverton Rd., NE, Silverton (503) 873-5463

Schreiner's Iris Gardens: 3625 Quinaby Rd.,(Brooks Exit off I-5) (503 393-3232

Swan Island Dahlias: Northwest 22nd Avenue, Canby (503) 266-7711

Wooden Shoe Tulip Gardens: 33814 S. Meridian, Woodburn (503)634-2243

✪, RR, DW, GS

SILVER FALLS STATE PARK

Silver Falls State Park boasts ten spectacular waterfalls. These falls range from 27 to 178 feet in height. The highest waterfall, South Falls, can be viewed from its highest point and then you can hike down a wooded trail to its base where you can walk under the falls. This largest park in Oregon contains 8,706 acres. There are many trails for hiking, picnic areas, horseback riding trails, and camp grounds. In the summer there are sometimes historical recreations and demonstrations.

Location: 20024 Silver Falls Hwy SE, Sublimity, OR (26 miles east of Salem), (503) 873-8681
$, RR, PT, DW, SB, R

PAUL JENSEN ARCTIC MUSEUM

Dr. Paul Jensen has been collecting the art and artifacts of the Arctic people for many years. As even remote villages in the Arctic began turning toward modern technology, he felt the need to preserve these people's way of life. The museum houses an extensive collection of Arctic arts and artifacts. An exhibit depicting the sights and sounds of an Arctic day is featured. Open Wednesday - Saturday 10-4. Closed January 1, Thanksgiving, and Christmas.

Location: 590 West Church Street on the campus of Western Oregon State College, Monmouth,
(503) 838-8468
✪, RR, DW, GS

FLYING M RANCH

The Flying M Ranch offers horseback riding and many hiking trails in an old West setting. The rustic log cabin provides food and lodging as well as a small museum. Stage coach and trail rides are popular features. The road in front of the ranch is the original 120 year-old stagecoach trail for journeys between the valley and the coast. The lodge also has a swimming pond, tennis, volleyball, horseshoes, and basketball.

Location: 23029 N.W. Flying M Road, Yamhill, OR (503) 662-3222
$$$, RR, PT, DW, R, GS

DETROIT LAKE RECREATION AREA

Detroit Lake offers boating, camping, fishing, water sports, picnicking, and hiking. This great recreation area boasts numerous parks which dot Detroit Lake's shoreline. Some are day-use only parks and others are for camping as well. Detroit Dam and Big Cliff Dam are in the area. Visitors can walk or drive across Detroit Dam. The Breitenbush and Santiam Rivers are nearby and also have numerous recreation opportunities including many forest campgrounds. The Breitenbush River road offers access to the Mt. Jefferson Wilderness area where use permits are required. These permits are available at the Willamette National Forest Ranger Station, across from Detroit Lake State Park. In winter there are many opportunities for cross-country skiers at Forest Service roads and Sno-Parks. Downhill skiers find good skiing at Hoodoo Ski Bowl at Santiam Pass. Downhill and cross-country skiers alike will enjoy the beauty of skiing in this area.

Location: on Highway 22
$, RR, PT, DW

AURORA COLONY MUSEUM

This five-building museum complex was part of the Old Aurora Colony, a communal German Christian society which flourished from 1856-1883. An old barn, containing original furniture, musical instruments, quilts, and tools is part of the complex. Other buildings in the complex are the Kraus Colony home, the 1876 Steinbach log cabin, a wash house, and a machine shed. A ten minute film is shown, giving visitors an overview of the colony. Open Tues - Sat. 10:00 - 4:00., Sunday: noon - 4:00.

Location: 15008 2nd Street, Aurora. (503) 678-5754
$$, RR, DW, GS

CHAMPOEG STATE PARK

This park is located on the bank of the Willamette River. It is at the site of Oregon's first provisional government. Besides picnicking, hiking, camping, and biking, there is a visitor's center with interpretive exhibits of the early American Indians, the fur trade, and other artifacts of Oregon's pioneer past. Also of interest, are two historic homes in the park. In July through early August, a spectacular pageant depicting Oregon's history, featuring over 75 live actors, is presented.

Location: 8239 Champoeg Rd., NE, St. Paul, OR (503) 678-1649

$, RR, PT, DW, I

HART'S REPTILE WORLD

For a great day in the country that kids will probably love, visit Hart's Reptile World. Bring a blanket and a picnic lunch and spend the day. The kids (and maybe you, too) will enjoy petting a 16 ft. tame python or giving a pat on the back to the T-shirted Wilbur, the Crocodile. There is also Sherman, the giant tortoise, who can be ridden by small children. Other reptiles are rattlesnakes, boa constrictors, cobras, iguanas, turtles, alligators, anacondas, king snakes, and monitors. The kids will enjoy being introduced to the fascinating world of reptiles. Open daily from 11 - 5.

Location: 11264 S. Macksburg Rd., Canby (503) 266-7236

$$ (Under 2 free), RR, DW, GS

MOLLALA MINIATURE STEAM TRAINS

Younger kids will enjoy a ride on a miniature steam train. Made to scale, the train travels on tracks which wind through woods, across bridges, and past picnic facilities. Open every Sunday (and holidays) from May - October, noon - 5.

Location: Shady Dell Park, Mollala, OR
❂, RR, PT, DW

FLOWER FARM - PHOENIX AND HOLLY RAILROAD

Take a ride on the 1/4 scale Phoenix and Holly Railroad. The tracks wind through fifteen acres of flower gardens. On weekends there is a petting zoo including horses, ponies, mules, goats, rabbits, and chickens. Board at the Mt. View Station for a ride on this train pulled by Sparky the Engine. There are special pumpkin train rides in October. A produce stand and flower shop are also located on the grounds of this agribusiness. Trains operate weekends only (when weather permits) from 11-6. Trains operate daily the last 3 weeks in October. There is also a special Christmas season.

Location: 2512 North Holly, 1 mile south of Canby (503) 266-3581
$, RR, PT, DW, SB, GS

Notes

Chapter 3

Explore Portland, Columbia Gorge, Mt. Hood Areas

3

Introduction

Portland, the city of Roses, is a beautiful river city built on the banks of both the Columbia and Willamette Rivers. A mild climate and unsurpassed beauty make this city very attractive to visitors. From most areas of the city, a spectacular view of Mt. Hood is visible on clear days and sometimes glimpses of snow-capped Mt. St. Helens and Mt. Adams are also seen.

From the internationally famous Rose Gardens to the new picturesque Tom McCall Waterfront Park, Portland delights the eye. The city has 200 beautiful parks, encompassing 10,000 acres. Portland is the only U.S. city with an extinct volcano (Mt. Tabor) within its city limits. The city boasts many large fountains such Ira's Fountain which is 18 feet high and 80 feet wide. On a warm day you may see youngsters and the young at heart jumping in the cool water. Some of the other fountains which are found in the city are Skidmore Fountain, Elk Fountain, Lovejoy Fountain, Shemanski Fountain, and the fountain at the new Rose Garden Sports Arena. Even drinking water fountains are found on many city streets.

If you happen to be in Portland in early June, the ten day Rose Festival features the Grand Floral Parade, much like the Pasadena Rose Parade, and the Starlight Parade. It also has boat and bicycle races, a fun center, tennis tournaments, art exhibits, and an opportunity to visit big naval ships which pull into port at that time. To see downtown Portland take a ride on its great public transportation system—Tri-Met buses or the MAX light rail. All rides are free in a 300 block section, known as "fareless square."

From Portland take Highway 84 for the trip along the magnificent Columbia River Gorge. On this route you will see spectacular Multnomah Falls, colorful wind surfers at Hood River, Bonneville Dam, and the Dalles Dam. On the way to The Dalles, stop and take a sternwheeler ride at Cascade Locks or take the interesting tours at Bonneville Dam. There are also parks along the route and the gorgeous scenery of the gorge and the Columbia River.

To the east of Portland take Highway 26 to Mt. Hood, a delightful place to visit in both winter and summer and to Oregonians, the "crown jewel" of the Cascades.

Within this small area of Oregon visitors may see a beautiful city, snow-capped mountains, a spectacular gorge, the mighty Columbia River, and towering Multnomah Falls. Among all this beauty, there are also many opportunities for families to enjoy museums, an exciting zoo, rides on excursion ships, ice skating, picnicking, hiking, and even a splash in one of Portland's famous fountains.

Pictures on page 49, clockwise from upper left: Metro Washington Park Zoo, Animal sculptures at Metro Washington Park Zoo, Discovery Zone

The Portland Area

ALPENROSE DAIRY

This is working dairy that welcomes visitors. There are cows, sheep, goats, and horses. There is a a western village and a museum with a large collection of dolls, antique toys, farm equipment, and old cars. The bicycle races held on summer weekends in the Velodrome are exciting to watch. The steep banks of the Velodrome make it popular for many levels of bicycle competition. Baseball games are also played on a field on the grounds. Special events occur throughout the year with the Storybook Lane at Christmas time especially popular. Open year round. Call for special events and times.

Location: 6149 SW Shattuck Road, (503) 244-1133
✪, RR, SB, GS

THE AMERICAN ADVERTISING MUSEUM

The history of advertising from 1683 to the present is exhibited in The American Advertising Museum. Old advertising posters, magazine and newspaper ads, and old radio and television commercials are part of the display. Adults might enjoy trying to find ads they remember and kids will enjoy the difference between today's and yesterday's advertisements. The museum is housed in an old theater building along with several ethnic restaurants. Open Wednesday - Sunday 11-5. Closed New Years Day, Thanksgiving and Christmas.

Location: 50 SW Second, Portland (503) 226-0000
$, RR, DW, R, GS

BEVERLY CLEARY SCULPTURE GARDEN FOR CHILDREN

If your kids are fans of Beverly Cleary's Ramona or Henry Huggins books (and what kids aren't) they will enjoy a visit to Grant Park where they can see the Beverly

Cleary Sculpture Garden for Children. The garden features a fountain with large bronze statues of Ramona, Henry Huggins, and Henry's dog, Ribsy. There are few monuments to children's literary characters anywhere in the world, so this is a rare opportunity to enjoy seeing sculptures of favorite book characters, created expressly for children. Let the kids tell you an adventure of Ramona or Henry or maybe you remember one yourself!

Location: In Grant Park near NE 33rd and Thompson St., Portland
✪, RR, PT, DW

CASCADE STERNWHEELERS

Sternwheelers were Portland's first mass transportation system, and a ride on one today will give you an exciting and fun way to see the "City of Roses". The paddle driven sternwheeler, Cascade Queen, and others like her, offer an hour and a half cruise around the harbor. Board the ship at the River Place Marina and enjoy a unique view of Portland. There is a snack bar on board the ship for those who prefer to do their sightseeing with a full tummy. Open year-round except for December when special holiday cruises may be chartered. Call for times of departures.

Location: 1200 NW Front Avenue, Suite 110, Portland (503) 223-3928
$$$, RR, SB,

CHILDREN'S MUSEUM

This hands-on museum for children gives kids the opportunity to play with water, "operate" in a hospital, shop in a grocery store, serve dinner in a restaurant, experiment with drawbridges, create with clay, and do many more things for creative fun. Also featured are art and history exhibits, shell collections, and international crafts.

There is an outdoor playground just outside in Lair Hill Park. The little ones will enjoy a break at the Children's Museum.

Location:3037 S. W. Second Avenue, Portland. (503) 823-2227
$$ (Free to children under 1), RR, DW, GS

JEFF MORRIS FIRE MUSEUM

If you're in the area let the kids see the old fire equipment at the Jeff Morris Fire Museum. The items in the museum are in a glass-enclosed area and visitors walk by in a covered area to see the antique fire equipment. Some of the items include: an 1863 hand-pumper fire engine, an 1870 steam-pumper engine, an 1870 hand-drawn ladder truck, and a 4,000 pound fire bell. Available anytime for a walk-by visit.

Location: 55 SW Ash at the north end of the Portland Fire Station, Portland
(503) 248-0203
✪

KIDD'S TOY MUSEUM

Beginning with antique cars and then expanding to antique toy cars, Frank Kidd developed an extensive collection of old toys. Among them are antique toy cars, toy tractors, taxicabs, motorcycles, toy bears, dolls, and a wonderful collection of mechanical banks. The collection also includes old license plates dating back to 1911 and old gas pumps. At present the collection is housed in an auto parts store, PARTS DISTRIBUTIONS, but in 1996 the owners hope to have their own building for their extensive toy collection at 1301 SE Grand, Portland. Open 8:00 - 5:30 Monday - Friday, 8:00 - 1:00 Saturday.

Location: 1300 SE Grand, Portland (503) 233-7807
✪

LLOYD CENTER

The Lloyd Center is basically a large shopping center, but it does have two things that make it a worthwhile stop for kids—Discovery Zone and an ice skating rink. Discovery Zone is an indoor playground for fitness and fun. Some of the activities are slides, foam mountains, ball baths, tunnels, and an obstacle course. The size of the child determines to some extent which activities can be pursued, so they need not worry about interference from bigger children. Kids can go from one activity to another at will. Arrangements for special parties can be made. (Another Discovery Zone is located at 8568 SW Apple Way, in Beaverton.) Some children might rather rent some ice skates and glide off on the ice in the beautiful ice pavilion. Both places are open year round and on most days of the week.

Location: Lloyd Center, Follow the Lloyd Center signs on I-84. (503) 288-2900
$$, RR, DW, SB, R, GS

METRO WASHINGTON PARK

Encompassing 332 acres, this largest of the Portland Parks, contains not only the usual picnic and play areas and jogging trails, but also the International Rose Test Gardens with over 10,000 roses. Even young children will enjoy a walk through these beautiful gardens and will enjoy reading the name of each rose. Below the gardens is a stage where free concerts are given throughout the summer. The Japanese Gardens, for which an admittance fee is required, are also in the park. These tranquil grounds are beautiful examples of oriental gardens. Hoyt Arboretum and the Vietnam Wall are also in the park.

Two statues in the park, "The Coming of the White Man" and "Sacajawea", commemorate Oregon's historic past. These statues were dedicated by Susan B. Anthony at the opening of the 1905 Lewis and Clark Exposition. A magnificent view of Mt. Hood can be seen from the upper level of the park. From this level you can also get a great view of Portland below.

Location: South from Burnside Rd. Main entrance at the head of Park Place (503) 823-2223
   ✪, RR, PT, DW

METRO WASHINGTON PARK ZOO

Portland's Metro Washington Park Zoo has been recently renovated and has some of the best zoo exhibits in the country. It's 61 acres provide plenty of room to see animals from almost every continent in natural settings. Dedicated to breeding and preserving endangered species, the zoo is home to the largest breeding herd of captive Asian elephants. The penguin exhibit is one of the nations best with simulated ocean waves and realistic  nesting areas. The newest exhibit, the African Rain Forest, houses crocodiles, bats, and pythons from West Africa. The Alaska Tundra exhibit houses wolves, grizzly bears, and other animals from Alaska. There is a large representation of animals native to Oregon. The kids will want you to buy them a ticket to ride on the zoo train which winds around the zoo and also past the Washington Park Rose Gardens and Japanese Gardens. During the summer months, there are special concerts and programs. At Halloween there are Zoo Boo train rides and at Christmas a festival of lights train ride. Come and plan to spend the day. Bring a lunch to eat at the picnic tables or buy something from the snack bars or restaurants. From antelopes to monkeys, to zebras, there is always something for the kids to enjoy at Metro Washington Park Zoo. The photo opportunities are many, so don't forget your camera! Open daily at 9:30. Closing times vary depending on season.

Location: In the Metro Washington Park, 4001 S.W. Canyon Rd., Portland, (503) 226-1561
$$, RR, PT, DW, SB, R, GS

NIKE TOWN

The kids will say, "Awesome" or "Cool!" when they visit Nike Town. More than just a place that sells sports equipment, it also has multi-media presentations, interactive displays, and sports memorabilia.

A knowledgeable staff will help make your visit even more of a treat.

Location: 930 SW 6th Avenue - corner of 6th Avenue & Salmon Streets, Portland.
(503) 221-NIKE
✪, RR, DW, GS

NORTH CLACKAMAS AQUATIC PARK

Let the kids spend an afternoon splashing and swimming at this water park which includes a wave pool, water slides, whirlpool, and wading pool.

Location: 7300 SE Harmony Road, Milwaukee (503) 650-3483
$$, RR, DW

OAKS PARK

Minutes from downtown Portland, is one of the city's oldest amusement parks. Its 44 fun-filled acres are located along the Willamette River. The park opened in 1905 at the time of the Lewis & Clark Exposition. Beautiful picnic areas and views of the city are but a part of this many-faceted park. The kids will enjoy the carnival rides which are varied and changing. There are adult thrill rides and also special thrill rides for kids, such as Tubs-O-Fun, Sky Fighter, C. P. Huntington Train Ride, Jump Cycles, Umbrella Car Ride, Kiddie Boats, etc. Children may also enjoy spending a few hours at the Oaks Roller Skating Rink. The rink has one of the nation's grandest Wurlitzer pipe organs which add to the skating fun. Another children's attraction in Oaks Park is the Ladybug Theater which presents participatory children's plays at different times. (Check for times - (503) 232-2346). The park is open weekends from mid-March until Memorial Day when it begins opening daily until Labor Day. Mondays are reserved for private parties only. The roller skating rink is open year-round.

Location: Located at the east end of the Sellwood Bridge (503) 233-5777

✪ (for park itself) $$ for rides and other attractions, RR, PT, DW, SB, GS

OREGON HISTORY CENTER

For less than the price of a movie, you and the kids can have fun learning about Oregon and its history. You may find yourself feeling like a time-traveler as you explore Oregon's past from prehistoric times to the present. There are both permanent and traveling exhibits to be seen in this beautiful building. The five floors housing the many exhibits are handicap accessible. Interactive videos are popular with the kids and there are many of them in this center. The museum store has interesting things at all price levels. The Oregon History Center is open Tuesday - Saturday 10:00 - 5:00. Sunday from 12:00 - 5:00.

Location: 1200 S. W. Park Avenue, Portland. (503) 306-5200

$, RR, DW, I, GS

OREGON MARITIME CENTER AND MUSEUM

This is an interesting museum with many exhibits, some hands-on activities, some working models, and explanatory videos. Kids might be interested in the exhibits of ships in bottles and will want to try to figure out how the ship got there. There are replicas of shipyards and docked nearby is an old sternwheeler, Sternwheeler Portland. This old sternwheeler is being restored and can be explored from stem to stern. Old deep-sea diving equipment and various ship models, are two of the other types of exhibits housed in this historic 1872 building. On a good day, bring a blanket to spread out on the nearby waterfront park grounds. Enjoy a picnic as you watch the boating and water skiing on the Willamette. Open summers from Wednesday - Sunday 11:00 - 4:00. In winter Friday - Sunday from 11:00 - 4:00.

Location: 113 SW Front Avenue, Portland (503) 224-7724
$, RR, DW, I, GS

OREGON MUSEUM OF SCIENCE & INDUSTRY (OMSI)

The new Oregon Museum of Science and Industry is a hands-on science museum. It has permanent and changing hands-on displays housed in six exhibit halls. Visitors are encouraged to touch the exhibits for real-life explorations. The visitor can learn about holograms, design and test a boat, rock and roll in earthquake or tornado simulations, play computer games, learn about space exploration through doing, and explore the mysteries of the universe such as black holes. Its Omnimax Theater has the largest film projection system ever made and its Murdock Sky Theater has exciting astronomy and laser light shows. The USS Blueback, a diesel submarine, is also part of the museum and visitors may tour this vintage submarine. This submarine was the last non-nuclear submarine to be built by the U. S. Navy. It was part of the Navy's submarine fleet for 31 years and was part of the Navy operations in many areas of the Pacific. The gift shop contains sel-dom-found items, usually science oriented, that will be of interest to both children and adults. The restaurant boasts a beautiful view of the Willamette River and of Waterfront Park. Open daily from 9:30 a.m. Closing time varies from 5:30 - 9:00. Closed on Christmas.

Location: 1945 S.E. Water Avenue, Portland. (503) 797-4000
$$$, RR, DW, R, GS

PORTLAND POLICE MUSEUM

Located in the top floor of the Justice Building, the Portland Police Museum contains old photos, badges, motorcycles, and other police memorabilia. There are also various crime displays. Open Monday - Thursday from 10 -3.

Location: 1111 SW 2nd, Portland   (503) 823-0019
✪, RR (down one floor), GS

PORTLAND SATURDAY MARKET

A visit to Portland wouldn't be complete without a visit to Portland's Saturday Market. The many ethnic food stands send out enticing aromas and the street musicians, jugglers, and mimes will catch your eye and entertain the kids. There are hundreds of booths where artists and crafters sell their interesting handcrafted creations. Metal sculptures, ceramics, furniture, clothes, jewelry, and toys are but a few of the items for sale at this colorful, friendly market place. Open every Saturday and Sunday from March through Christmas Eve, Saturday from 10:00 - 5:00, Sunday from 11:00 - 4:30.

Location: Under the west end of the Burnside Bridge, (503) 222-6072
✪, RR, SB, GS

SAMTRAK

From May until October you can take the kids from OMSI to Oaks Park or ride from the park to OMSI on SAMTRAK. There is also a one-hour round trip offered on this one-car train. The train seats one-hundred people and wends its way along the Willamette River, leaving from Spokane Street on the hour, and from OMSI on the half hour with a stop at Oaks Park each way. Operates Wednesday - Sunday during the summer months, weekends during September - October. Check for times and special rates.

Location: Boards at OMSI 1945 SE Water Ave, Oaks Park - SE Oaks Park Dr. (across from Park entrance) or Spokane Street under east end of Sellwood Bridge. (503) 659-5452
$$, RR

TRYON CREEK STATE PARK

This wonderful park, although in the city, retains its original feeling of being in a dense forest, The sights and sounds of the city seem far away. There are many beautiful hiking trails, some of which are handicap accessible. There are also horseback riding trails and bicycle trails. The nature house in the park is interesting in itself, with its many displays, a library, occasional programs, and a nature-emphasis gift shop. Over 80 species of birds and many small mammals - including beavers are at home in the park.

Location: Off I-5, Terwilliger Blvd., SW Portland. (503) 653-3166
✪, RR, PT, DW, GS

WORLD FORESTRY CENTER

Would your kids like to have a conversation with a tree? At the World Forestry Center there is a talking tree, an old growth forest display, and a multi-media presentation on the forests of the world. There is also the Burnett Collection of Petrified Woods, featuring wood from the time of the dinosaurs. The Forestry Center also operates a demonstration forest located 25 miles south of Portland in Wilsonville. It features a hiking trail, log bunkhouses, an authentic fire lookout tower and a visitor's center. If you would like to visit this demonstration forest, check at the Forestry Center for more information. The World Forestry Center is located in Metro Washington Park near the Metro Washington Park Zoo so you may wish to visit both on the same day. Open every day except Christmas. Summer 9:00 - 5:00 and after Labor Day 10:00 - 5:00.

Location: 4033 SW Canyon Rd., Portland. (503) 228-1367

$ (Outdoor exhibits are free, children under 2 years free), RR, DW, GS

Oregon City Area

Oregon City was officially the end of the arduous Oregon Trail and there is much to commemorate the event in present-day Oregon City. The town was built on two levels and to make access to both levels easier, in 1913 the early townspeople built a water-run elevator. This elevator was replaced by an electricity driven elevator in 1954. This elevator is one of the few municipal elevators in the world. Take the 30 second ride on this unique elevator and then see the rest of historic Oregon City.

OREGON CITY MUNICIPAL ELEVATOR

The Oregon City Municipal Elevator rises ninety feet from lower Oregon City to the upper business and residential area of the city. At the top of the elevator is an enclosed observation deck with a panoramic view of the city and the Willamette River. Under the windows of the deck are many murals depicting pioneer life and historic events of the era. The elevator operates from 6:45 a.m. - 7:00 p.m. on Monday - Saturday, 11:00 a.m. - 7:00 p.m. on Sundays.

Location: 7th and Main, Oregon City
✪

CARNEGIE CENTER/CHILDREN'S MUSEUM

A three-block walk from the top of the municipal elevator (see above) will take you to the Carnegie Center, a small but child-pleasing children's museum. The museum is housed in the lower level of the Carnegie Center and children may play on a fire engine, board a motorcycle, teach school, grocery shop, "cook" and serve a meal in a restaurant, or go to a credit union or the post office. There are also exhibits of snakes, lizards, and shells. Above the children's area is a delightful art gallery and a snack bar where you can get a cup of tea or coffee to take with you as you watch the kids. Outside this former Carnegie Library there is a wading pool and play equipment. Open M - F 8:00 a.m. - 7:00 p.m., Saturday 10:00 - 6:00.

Location: 606 John Adams Street, Oregon City (503) 557-9199
$, RR, PT, DW, SB, GS

CLACKAMAS COUNTY HISTORICAL SOCIETY MUSEUM

This large, relatively new museum offers magnificent views of the Willamette River and Willamette Falls, as well as a large collection of memorabilia. The museum's collection is divided into sections dealing with religion, agriculture, education, architecture, government, industry, health and medicine, and Native Americans. Each section includes many exhibits and replicas of old buildings or businesses, such as the old pharmacy in the health and medicine section. An historical time line helps visitors interpret the collection and put the events in proper perspective. Of special interest to kids will be the old toys, beautiful dolls, children's books, children's clothing, and a section of baby dishes. A pioneer wagon filled with objects usually taken on the Oregon Trail is interesting to most visitors. A 20 minute video about the pioneer woman can be viewed. Open: Monday - Friday from 10:00 - 4:00, Saturday and Sunday from 1:00 - 5:00. Closed New Years Day, Thanksgiving, and Christmas.

Location: 211 Tumwater Drive & 99E, Oregon City. (503) 655-5574
$, RR, DW, I, GS

END OF THE OREGON TRAIL INTERPRETIVE CENTER

Feel like a pioneer on the Oregon Trail as you experience the multimedia dramatization with surround-sound

that awaits you at the End of the Oregon Trail Interpretive Center. The unique wagon-shaped buildings are set in a natural Northwest surrounding. They house extensive exhibits of the pioneers and reflect their dreams as they headed West. During the guided tour, guides try to encourage children's active participation in the presentation. Allow at least an hour for the guided tour/multimedia presentation. Outside, visitors can stroll the gardens which represent the beauty and bounty that awaited the pioneers in the "land of Eden's Gate." At times visitors can see live demonstrations of pioneer crafts such as candle-making, soap making, weaving, etc. An outdoor amphitheater features live performances and demonstrations of pioneer and Indian life. Open Monday through Saturday 9:00 - 6:00 P.M, Sunday 10:00 - 5:00.

Location: 1726 Washington St., Oregon City. (503) 657-9336
$$, RR, DW, GS

JOHN INSKEEP ENVIRONMENTAL LEARNING CENTER

Bring a picnic lunch and enjoy eating it on a recycled picnic table located on a former industrial site that has been restored as a beautiful nature center. There are hiking trails, wildlife habitat, duck-filled ponds, and a small exhibit pavilion (pavilion charges a small fee). Also on the grounds is the Haggert Observatory, which is open from 7:30 - 10:00 on clear nights on Wednesdays, Thursdays, and Fridays. A fee is charged. The Environmental Learning Center grounds are open from 8 a.m. to dusk daily.

Location: At the Beavercreek entrance of Clackamas Community College, (503) 657-6958 exit. 2351
✪, RR, PT, I, GS

The Columbia Gorge

BONNEVILLE DAM AND FISH HATCHERY

Take time to spend an hour or several hours at the Bonneville Dam and Fish Hatchery. The pleasant grounds, which include picnic areas, are inviting after a hot ride. Both the dam and the fish hatchery are interesting and informative.

The Bradford Island Visitor Center has an underwater viewing area where migrating fish can be seen moving up a fish ladder. Other features are an observation deck and audio-visual presentations.

Adjacent to the dam is the Bonneville fish hatchery. The hatchery has ponds containing sturgeon and trout.

You can walk around the various ponds and see the fish being fed. Open daily 9:00-5. Closed January 1, Thanksgiving, and Christmas.

Location: Take Exit 40, off I-84. (541) 374-8820
✪, RR, PT, DW, I, SB

THE DALLES

The city of The Dalles is an old and an interesting one. A series of murals is being painted on the sides of many of the buildings. The murals tell the story of the Native Americans, fur trappers, and pioneers who make up the history of the area. Walk the streets and see if older children can tell the story the murals depict.

Other things in or near The Dalles which might be interesting include a city park, a Stonehenge Replica, The Fort Dalles Museum, and a riverfront park.

Some specific things for children to enjoy in The Dalles are listed below.

THE WONDER WORKS CHILDREN'S MUSEUM

The Wonder Works Children's Museum is being constantly improved and expanded. It is staffed by volunteers and financed by the small admission price. The museum is located in downtown The Dalles at the present, but a new location is being sought.

Though small, this museum has many fascinating things for children to do and is completely "hands-on". Activities change often but include play activities such as a stage with puppets to use, a grocery store, a play house, science activities, and play areas. There is a special room for toddlers where older children are not permitted.

Parents are admitted free of charge and are expected to accompany their children. Come for a short time or stay as long as you wish. It will be a welcome break for kids, especially ones from approximately 18 months to 8 years. Open Tues - Sat. 10:00 - 5:00. Closed holidays.

Location: 419 East 2nd Street, The Dalles, (541) 296-2444
$, RR, DW

THE DALLES DAM AND TOUR TRAIN RIDE

Tour The Dalles Dam by train. During the summer months a small train takes visitors around the dam. Riders can get off the train and take the inside tour of the dam and then board the train again and get off at a grassy, shaded park where there are picnic tables, rest rooms, and drinking water. The interpretive center at the dam includes Lewis and Clark and Oregon Trail histories.

Be sure to notice the Native American petroglyths which are located at the entrance to the dam. Open daily 9-5:30 during the summer months. It is open 10:00 - 4:30, Monday through Wednesday during the spring and fall.

Location: Off I-84 at the east end of The Dalles (541) 296-1181
✪, RR, PT, DW

MT. HOOD SCENIC RAILROAD

Linking the Columbia Gorge to the foothills of Mt. Hood, is the Mt. Hood Scenic Railroad. The railroad is located less than an hour from Portland on Interstate 84. The railroad was built in 1906 and retains its turn-of-the-century feeling. The train departs from Hood River at the Mt. Hood Railroad Depot, and climbs steadily up the beautiful Hood River Valley. The kids will enjoy the ride in the old-fashioned train and the whole family will enjoy spectacular views of the Cascades. Food is served on the train at an additional cost. When the train reaches Mt. Hood at Parkdale, there is usually time to go into the Hutson Museum before the train makes the return trip. This museum boasts many Native American artifacts and a very large rock and mineral collection. In September - October the fall foliage is a plus, and the blossoms of Hood River's orchards are breath-taking in the spring. Open April - October. The morning train usually leaves at 10:00 a. m. and returns at 2:00 P.M. The afternoon train leaves at 3:00 p.m. and returns at 7:00 p.m. Calling for reservations and times is advised.

Location: 110 Railroad Avenue, Hood River (541) 386-3556
$$$, RR, DW, SB. At the depot are RR, PT, DW, I, GS

MULTNOMAH FALLS

The 620 foot Multnomah Falls is a "must see" for most people visiting Oregon. It is the most visited spot in the state. After the "Ohs and Ahs!" kids can stretch their legs as they view the highest falls in Oregon. It is the second highest falls in the United States. There are trails to climb for those who wish to spend time at the falls and the scenery is spectacular. Staying on the trails and using caution on them is always advised. An interpretive center is found at the base of the falls. It has historical, biological, and geological displays. Relax and stay cool at this beautiful spot.

Location: 31 miles east of Portland, on I-84 (503) 695-2376
✪, RR, DW, I, R, SB, GS

THE STERNWHEELER COLUMBIA GORGE

The Sternwheeler, Columbia Gorge, departs from Cascade Locks. The two-hour cruise is narrated and includes interesting legends of the area. This section of the Columbia Gorge is considered one of the best wind surfing areas in the world. Children and adults will both enjoy watching the wind surfers operate their brightly colored sailboards. From the deck, you can see historic Indian fishing sites and beautiful scenery. Brunch and dinner cruises are also available. While waiting to ride on the sternwheeler, there are things to do in Cascade Marine Park. In the park are playgrounds, picnic tables, gift shop and a museum. Cruises operate daily from June to October.

Location: Cascade Locks Marina Park, Exit 44 off I-84 (503) 223-3928
$$$, RR, PT, DW, I, SB, GS

Mt. Hood Area

Take Highway 26 out of Portland to visit beautiful Mt. Hood, or if you are already on I-84 you may wish to take Exit 64 to highway 35. Picture perfect views of the white-capped mountain are seen as you drive these highways. While the winter skiing, snowboarding, snowmobiling, and sledding are the Mt. Hood activities that first come to mind, there are also many things to do in the summer. A visit to picturesque Timberline Lodge, built in the 1930s, is alone worth the trip.

OREGON CANDY FARM

If you need or would like a stop on your way up to Mt. Hood, you may enjoy a stop at the Oregon Candy Farm where over a hundred varieties of candy are for sale. You may get to see some of the candy being cooked, but you will definitely get a free piece of candy! The candy is priced from 10 cents up. Open 9 - 5, Monday - Friday, noon - 5 weekends. Closed on holidays.

Location: Highway 26 on the way to Mt. Hood (503) 668-5066
✪, GS

MT. HOOD SKI BOWL

Mt. Hood Skibowl has a bowlful of activities for kids in both winter and summer. In the summer ride the sky chair to the top of Skibowl Peak. When you arrive have the camera ready and let the kids try their hand at taking a great picture of the spectacular view from the top. When you're ready to descend, board the sky chair again or hike down one of the trails. Take a thrilling ride on the Northwest's only alpine slide. The slide is fun for the whole family as you zip through alpine meadows to the base of the mountain. Children from the age of six can probably enjoy the ride. The speed of the ride can be controlled by a simple lever. Older kids will get a thrill from a ride on Skibowl's Can-Am cart race course. They can race with the wind as they maneuver the turns, dips, twists, and curves of this exciting race course. There are also bicycle trails and horse or pony riding. In the winter there are special inner tube hills for both kids and adults. There is also a Snowboard Park for experienced snowboarders. You can downhill ski both night and day. Kids under six may ski free with an adult. Lessons are available for all levels of skiing and equipment may be rented.

Location: Government Camp Oregon, (503) 272-3206
$$$ (depending on activity), RR, DW, R, GS

MT. HOOD MEADOWS AND MULTIPOR

Mt. Hood Meadows offers Kidski Programs and a Snowboard camp as well as traditional skiing. Solarski operates from late May to early July for skiing and snowboarding.

Location: Take I-84 to Exit 64 in Hood River, Follow Highway 35 to Entrance (If you are already on Highway 26, take Highway 35 from 26 to entrance) (503) 227-7669
$$$, RR, R, GS

TIMBERLINE

Timberline offers several children's skiing and snowboarding programs including the SKIwee program, a supervised full-day program to help children learn to ski or snowboard. The lodge is spectacular with its huge timbers, wooden sculptures, and gigantic fireplace. Built in the 1930's it is a work of art and even boasts a resident St. Bernard dog. Summer activities include hiking, picnicking, and lifts to the top  of the mountain. The alpine flowers and the beautiful views of Mt. Hood are constant invitations to use the camera. The grounds and lodge may be visited without charge.

Location: Highway 35 off either I-84 or Highway 26 (503) 272-3311
$$$, RR, DW , SB, R, GS

RAINBOW TROUT FISHING FARM

If you leave Mt. Hood early enough, you and the kids may want to stop at the Rainbow Trout Fishing Farm where everybody catches a fish. The cost depends on the size of the fish caught, with a six-inch fish being 50 cents and on up. Tackle can be furnished. Open seven days a week from February - October, 8 - dusk.

Location: 52560 E. Sylvan Dr., Sandy, OR - On highway 26 between mileposts 32 - 33. (503) 622-5223
$, RR, PT, DW, SB, I, GS

Notes

Chapter 4

Explore
Central
Oregon

4

Introduction

Central Oregon is truly a smorgasbord of activities for children and adults. In the summer hiking, bicycling, fishing, rafting, swimming, and mountain climbing, are available. In winter there are cross-country skiing, sledding, snow boarding, snowmobile riding, ice skating and even a ride by dog sled!

Besides the sports activities there are numerous things to see indoors. There are many museums in the area, including the famous The High Desert Museum with both things to see and things to do.

The area abounds with fresh water lakes where you may hike, fish, paddle boat, canoe, or swim. The Deschutes and the Santiam Rivers also provide these opportunities as well as thrilling white water rafting trips.

The sightseeing opportunities are also varied. The snow-capped mountains, which include Mt. Bachelor, Mt. Jefferson, Mt. Washington, The Three Sisters, and Three-Fingered Jack provide a magnificent backdrop to clear blue lakes, Ponderosa and jack pine forests, and lava and rock formations. Herds of llama and elk may be seen as you travel through the area.

There are numerous resorts in the area such as Sunriver, Kahneeta, Inn of the Seventh Mountain, and

Eagle Crest, but if resorts are too expensive for your taste there are motels at every price range available in the Bend and Redmond areas. There are also a variety of campgrounds. In the busiest tourist seasons, summer and winter, you will want to secure lodging several days ahead or plan to arrive early in the day.

You will find excellent restaurants in the resorts and in Bend, Sisters, and Redmond.

Visit the Bend Visitor Center, 63085 N. Highway 97, Bend, for more information. The places listed below are certainly not all of the available things to do. We have tried to list the things that are of particular interest to children, but there are numerous other things to do and places to go that might be fun or exciting to your own family. Explore Central Oregon. You will be glad you did!

Photos on page 73 from upper left clockwise: Petersen Rock Garden, Sunriver biking trails, Sisters, Lava Cast Forest. Center: Mt. Bachelor Cross Country Trails.

Bend Area

DESCHUTES HISTORICAL CENTER

An historical museum, The Deschutes Historical Center, is located in downtown Bend. It contains a replica of a pioneer schoolroom, other pioneer memorabilia, and Indian artifacts. It's location in "Old" Bend is also a plus. Take a walk in this interesting area and perhaps have lunch at The Pine Tree Tavern, which is not a tavern but an excellent restaurant. It's name is due to the large pine tree which grows in the dining area. The Deschutes Historical Center is open Tuesday through Saturday, 10 a.m. - 4:30 p. m.

Location: 129 NW Idaho, Bend
✪, RR

DRAKE PARK

Drake Park is located in downtown Bend. There are eleven acres of lawn and trees bordering the Deschutes River. Children enjoy feeding the plentiful ducks and there is also a playground located nearby. The Pole, Pedal, Paddle competition for kids is held annually at the park in May.

Location: Borders Riverside Boulevard in downtown Bend
✪, RR, PT, DW

FUNNY FARM

Does your family like things that are different? If they do, take time to drive to the Funny Farm! Kids can explore the the Yellow Brick Road or visit a bowling ball garden. They can feed the various farm animals that are on the farm. While the kids are exploring , adults may want to visit Buffet Flats, a quaint antique shop on the grounds.

You may wonder if "the owners are simple-minded or just plain wacko", but the experience is certainly unique. Their brochure states, "All well-mannered adults and supervised children welcome!" Open 10-5, 7 days a week except for Christmas.

Location: 64990 Deschutes Market Road, Bend (541)-389-6391
✪, RR,PT, GS

HIGH DESERT MUSEUM

Kids from 5 - 80 will enjoy the nationally acclaimed, HIGH DESERT MUSEUM. The 150 acre High Desert Museum is surrounded by the Deschutes National Forest. There are many "hands-on" activities for the young or young at heart. Twenty acres of nature trails surround the museum. On the trail visitors can see an historic sawmill, a settler's cabin, a Sheepherder's Wagon and a Forestry Learning Center. Porcupines, river otters, and birds of prey can be seen in natural settings. Part of the trail leads past a trout stream which meanders through the ground. Interpretive talks are featured throughout the day. Inside the museum, visitors can enjoy western art, Native American artifacts, and take a walk back into time in the Eric A . Chiles Center. In the center, sights and sounds create a setting where kids and adults can meet the natives, explorers, and settlers of this land. Special exhibits and pioneer history demonstrations are featured. In the Desertarium mice, bats, owls, reptiles, and other forms of desert life can be seen. There is also a movie theater, showing films of the area. Spend an hour or two, or an entire day at the High Desert Museum without getting bored! Open 9-5 daily except Jan. 1, Thanksgiving and Christmas.

Location: 6 miles south of Bend on Highway 97. (541) 382-4754
$$ (Children 4 & under - Free), RR, DW, R, GS

ICE SKATING RINKS

Ice skating rinks are located at The Inn of the Seventh Mountain and at the Sunriver Village. Skates can be rented and there is a fee for skating. You need not be a guest to skate. In the summer the skating rink at Sunriver is used for miniature golf. Some of the parks in the area also have ice skating ponds. These are free but you must have your own skates, except at Shevlin Park where skates can be rented.

Location: The Inn of the Seventh Mountain and Sunriver Village, Also various parks in and around Bend.
$, RR

LAVA BUTTE AND LAVA LANDS VISITOR CENTER

Lava Butte is a volcanic cinder cone. A paved road leads to the top where a beautiful view of the Cascade Mountains can be seen. Park at the bottom of Lava Butte and a bus will take you to the top. At the top there is a working ranger station where watch is kept for forest fires. This is usually open to visitors who can see the Cascade Mountains from the windows. Kids of all ages enjoy feeding the tame chipmunks and ground squirrels which frequent the area. Open daily, late spring through early fall.

Interpretive trails wind around the crater and over the lava flow and through the adjoining pine forest. Guided Tours are also available. The Lava Land Visitor Center contains displays and there are slide shows to describe the history of the area. There is a naturalist on duty. Phone for hours.

Location: 11 miles south of Bend, on Highway 97. (541) 388-5664
✪, RR, DW, I

LAVA CAST FOREST

Free maps are available for a self-guided hike through the Lava Cast Forest. As you walk on the mile long trail, you can begin to understand what happened at the 6000 year-old Newberry Crater. The forests' stone trees were formed when a lava flow covered the trees. When the lava cooled, it left tree casts where the trees had burned away. Children might enjoy climbing inside the casts or locating the items listed on the map. Bring the camera and let the kids try capturing the beauty amidst the ruins of a once-thriving forest.

Location: South of Bend, exit from Highway 97, opposite the Sunriver exit.

✪, RR, PT, I

LAVA RIVER CAVE

Rent a lantern (during the summer months) or bring your own and travel into a lava tube. The nearly mile-long tube, which ranges in height from approximately 4 feet to 40 feet, was formed from lava which cooled, leaving the tube. Pioneers kept their food in these tubes because the temperature is a constant 40 degrees. Since this is cool, plan to wear comfortable walking shoes and warm clothes. If you enjoy this cave, you might also enjoy exploring on your own other lava caves such as Skeleton Cave, Wind Cave, and Arnold Ice Cave.

Location: 12 miles south of Bend on U.S. 97
$, RR, DW, PT

MOUNT BACHELOR

Although best known for its great skiing, Mount Bachelor is also of interest in the summer. The summer season begins on Memorial Day with lift rides to the 9,065 foot summit. From the summit there is a spectacular view of three states and the Central Oregon Cascade Mountains. Other summer services are picnic sites and mountain bike rentals. In the winter Mount Bachelor offers downhill skiing, served by ten lifts. There are also 3,200 acres of glades and groomed trails for cross country skiing. Instructors are available. Skis can be rented in the rental shop. There is a fully-licensed day care center and special slow-skiing areas on the slopes for children. Kids under six may ski free. Open daily.

Location: 22 miles west of Bend on the Cascade Lakes Highway. 1-800-829-2442

✪ - to visit $$$ for skiing, ski rentals etc., RR, PT, DW, SB, R, GS

NEWBERRY NATIONAL VOLCANIC MONUMENT

The Newberry Crater is a huge caldera. Within the caldera is Paulina Lake and East Lake. These lakes are separated by cinder cones and a large obsidian flow. The area abounds with geological and natural beauty. Within the 50,000 acre monument you will find obsidian fields, lakes, lava formations, and waterfalls. You can drive around the lakes or drive to Paulina Peak for a panoramic view. During the summer there are campfire programs and nature walks led by naturalists. The helpful Newberry Crater Visitor Center is open daily from late June - Labor Day.

Location: 24 miles south of Bend, 13 miles east of US 97 on County Rd. 21. (541) 385-7439

$, RR, PT, DW, I

SHEVLIN PARK

Winter ice skating at the Hatchery Pond is one feature of the five hundred acres comprising Shevlin Park. Skates can be rented for the ice skating. In the summer months visitors can enjoy the many trails and picnic areas. Tumalo Creek runs

through the tree-shaded park. At Halloween a "haunted train" takes passengers on an exciting ride in Shevlin Park.

Location: Five miles west of Bend on Shevlin Park Road
○, RR, PT, DW

SUNRIVER

While Sunriver is a resort with many rentals available, you need not be a guest there to enjoy its recreational opportunities. There are 35 miles of paved bike trails in Sunriver and several places where you may rent bicycles with or without child carriers. Horseback rides and pony rides are available there. You can take a canoe or kayak and float down the Deschutes River. The companies which rent the equipment for the float will take you to the place where you enter the river. When your trip down the river is complete, there will be someone waiting to pick you up and take you back to the marina. There are many shops and an ice skating rink in the winter and miniature golf in the summer.

Location: 16 miles from Bend off Highway 97
○ (to visit) $$$ (for activities), RR, DW, SB, R, GS

SUNRIVER NATURE CENTER

The Sunriver Nature Center features nature activities, astronomy programs at its observatory, and living and inanimate history displays. There are both indoor and out-door things to see and do. Live animals from the area can be seen. There is a rehabilitation area where injured animals are healed and prepared to return to the wild.

Location: 18 miles south of Bend, off Highway 97. Take the Sunriver exit and follow signs to marina, airport, and stables. (541) 593-4394
$, RR, DW

TRAIL OF DREAMS SLED DOG RIDES

If you should be in the Bend area in the winter and want a ride you will remember, take a dog sled ride! The ride begins at Sunrise Lodge on Mt. Bachelor. The riders' excitement grows as the dog sled trainer takes the professional dog sled dogs from their cages, one by one, and hitches them to the dog sled. The lead dog is the last dog to be hitched to the sled. Then the anchor is removed and the sled is off on an exciting ride looping from the lodge to Baby Dutchman Flats, through the forest, into a meadow and back to the lodge.

Location: Mt. Bachelor, 22 miles west of Bend on Cascade Lakes Highway. 1-800-829-2442

$$$

WET WILLIE'S BUMPER BOATS

Wet Willie's Bumper Boats is something the kids will love! Besides bumping the boats, much like the way bumper cars are used, the kids can also participate in water balloon wars. Other available activities are batting cages and miniature golf.

Location: 61116 S. Highway 97, Bend (541) 388-2937

$$, RR, PT

WHITEWATER RAFT TRIPS

There are several whitewater rafting businesses in and around Bend. These companies offer various options for whitewater rafting. Usually children must be at least seven years of age. Most trips

are three hours long but day trips which include lunch are also available. All equipment is furnished and transportation is furnished to and from the river. Pickup locations are in both Bend and Sunriver. Wear clothing which will dry quickly for you will surely get wet! Check with the various businesses to see which ones offer the best children's trips.

Location: Check with Bend Visitors' Center for the location of the various whitewater rafting businesses.
(541) 382-3221
$$$

Redmond Area

KID ZONE

A great place for kids to let off steam, The Kid Zone, offers various attractions geared to active participation. Unlimited use of the play area is included in the admission. A video arcade will appeal to older kids. There is no admission charge for adults. During the summer months there are many outdoor activities. These include a train and a ferris wheel for the toddler set, and miniature golf and bumper boats for older children. An adjoining small museum contains vintage cars, baseball and movie star memorabilia, and other items of interest to kids.

Location: 3290 S. Highway 97, Redmond   (541) 923-0000
$$, RR, PT, DW, R, GS

OPERATION SANTA CLAUS

Near Redmond the Operation Santa Claus ranch raises reindeer which are used all over the country for Christmas activities. See the reindeer and learn about them. There is a sleigh available for taking pictures. Open 365 days a year for self-guided tours. During Christmas season there may be special events.

Location: 4355 West Highway 126, Redmond, (541)548-8910

✪, RR, GS

PETERSEN ROCK GARDENS

Near Bend and Redmond is a fascinating attraction that kids of all ages will enjoy. Peterson Rock Gardens was built by Rasmus Petersen as a hobby . He built miniature bridges, replicas of famous buildings, towers, and terraces using thousands of different kinds of rocks. Guessing at the names of the various buildings or trying to identify the various rocks used in their construction, is fun and interesting. Rock bridges cross over a stream where ducks are paddling. Peacocks and peahens stroll the grounds. They are unafraid of humans and let children and adults come close to them. Trees, green grass, and flowers add to the enjoyment of a visit to PETERSEN ROCK GARDENS. Open 365 Days a year, 9 to dusk. The grounds and museum are supported by donations at the entrance gate.

Location: Midway between Bend and Redmond, off U.S. 97

✪, RR, PT, GS

SMITH ROCK STATE PARK

North of Redmond on U.S. 97 near the small town of Terrebonne, is Smith Rock State Park. This beautiful park consists of 641 acres, containing the awe-inspiring rock spires of the Crooked River Canyon. Two miles of developed trails wind through the rock climbing areas. There are additional hiking possibilities on rough trail routes, and visitors should use these and the developed trails and not try to make trails of their own. The rock-climbing at Smith Rock is popular with rock climbers from around the world. Both children and adults will enjoy seeing these experienced rock climbers. Wildlife can also be seen here, especially deer, birds, and geese. Park regulations are posted at the entrance to the trails. There may be seasonal

closings for rock climbers but the park itself is open. In the late fall, winter, and early spring there is no charge, but during the summer there may be a day-use charge.

Location: North of Redmond, off Highway 97.
$, RR, PT, DW

Sisters Area

HEAD WATERS OF THE METOLIUS

Take a hike on well-paved trails to the head waters of the Metolius River. The trail leads through tall Ponderosa pines. In one widened part of the trail amateur and professional photographers can take a beautiful picture of snow-capped Mt. Jefferson, framed on either side by the

trees. Let the kids try to get a picture of the beautiful mountain. Then continue on the trail until you reach the spot where the crystal clear waters of the Metolius emerge from the ground in a thirty to forty foot wide area. No one is sure of the water's origin but speculate it may come from Crater Lake or some other of the many lakes in the region. There are picnic areas near the parking lot. If you continue a few miles down the road to Camp Sherman, you will find a country store near a stream. Children will enjoy standing on the bridge and feeding the giant trout which swim in the sparkling clear water below the bridge.

Location: 35 miles northwest of Bend. Forest Road 14, off Highway 20

✪, RR, PT, DW

WIZARD FALLS FISH HATCHERY

If you continue down Forest Road 14 from the region of the Metolius Headwaters, you will find the Wizard Falls Fish Hatchery. Kids are allowed to feed the fish in the holding ponds. Wildlife is abundant and you may see deer, otter, geese and ducks in the area and the area surrounding the hatchery. If you like fishing, the Metolius is famous for fly fishing and there are fishing spots above and below the hatchery.

Location: 35 miles northwest of Bend on Highway 20 and then on Forest Road 14.

✪, RR, I

Other Areas

A. R. BOWMAN MEMORIAL MUSEUM

This museum located in a 1910 former bank building, houses a fine collection of items. Exhibits of old and interesting things include toys, dolls, old uniforms, antique radios and telephones, furniture, saddles, branding irons and more. The bank setting, with all its old furnishings, make for a novel arrangement and an enjoyable, educational visit. Open every day from June - August. Open Monday - Saturday for the rest of the year. Closed January, February, and holidays. 10-5 M-F, 11-5 Saturday.

Location: 246 North Main Street, Prineville (541) 447-3715
✪, RR

COVE PALISADES STATE PARK

Cove Palisades State Park is located on Lake Billy Chinook and is great for water sports. Here three rivers, the Crooked River, the Deschutes, and the Metolius come together to form the huge reservoir. Around the lake are three recreation areas, providing boating, swimming, fishing, and water sports opportunities. The swimming area is roped-off and there are some bath houses. Houseboats may be rented for water exploration. Jet skis may be rented at the marina. There are hiking trails or you may take the Cove Palisades Tour Route for a spellbinding view of the area. Down river Lake Simtustus also offers water sports activities. Open from May - October.

Location: 10 miles southwest of Madras off US 97. (541) 546-3412
$, RR, PT, DW, SB

PINE MOUNTAIN OBSERVATORY

Pine Mountain Observatory is known as a fine observatory. Sky-viewing is best at night and if you wish to visit, call ahead for reservations. There are 15, 24, and 32 inch telescopes at the observatory, which is the only major observatory in the Northwestern United States. The trip to Pine Mountain is also an enjoyable day trip. The countryside is beautiful and when you reach the area of the observatory, you may see hang gliders gliding from the mountain. The view from the Pine Mountain is spectacular. Observatory is open May 1 - Sept 30 on Friday and Saturday evenings. Call after 3:00 for reservations.

Location: 35 miles east of Bend. Take U.S. Highway 20 to Millican, then turn nine miles south of marked road.

$ (for observatory), RR, PT, DW

SHANIKO GHOST TOWN

Getting to Shaniko from Bend is quite a long drive but an interesting one for older children. Shaniko is a ghost town with but a few remaining residents. In Shaniko you can stay in the old hotel there which is furnished as it was when the town was a flourishing hub of  activity. If you don't wish to spend the night , you may ask to see the quaint rooms in this old hotel. While in the town you can see many varieties of old wagons and vintage cars. The ghost town still has an old schoolhouse, church, and jail which you may go into. A summer festival, Shaniko Days, is held the first weekend in August. It provides an exciting weekend of stage coach rides, shootouts in the street, music, dance hall troupes, a barbecue dinner, and many booths selling crafts.

Location: North of Bend on Highway 18
❂, R, GS

THE MUSEUM AT WARM SPRINGS

Dedicated to preserving the heritage of the tribes of the Warm Springs Indians, this museum has over 7500 square feet of exhibits. These exhibits include photographs, artifacts, films, and interactive displays. Visitors entering the song chamber are surrounded by traditional tribal singing and drumming. There are also reconstructions of various tribal dwellings. Art exhibits feature work of Native American artists from the Pacific Northwest. In the summer there are often demonstrations of dancing, storytelling, drum making, beadwork, and basketry. Open 10:00 - 5:00 daily. Closed New Years, Thanksgiving, & Christmas.

Location: 2189 Highway 26 (541) 553-3331

$$ (Children under 4 are free and there is also a special family rate), RR, DW, GS

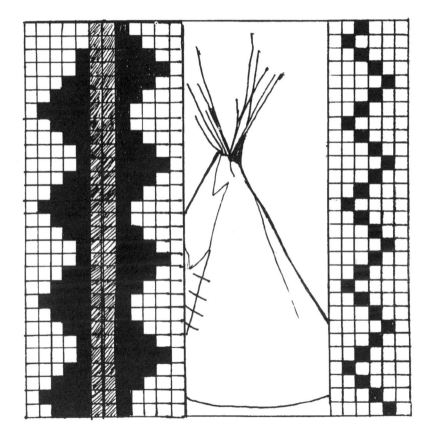

Notes

Chapter 5

Explore
Eastern
Oregon

5

Introduction

Get the feel of the Old West as you explore Eastern Oregon. The region boasts mountain peaks, awesome geologic rock formations, thousands of acres of sagebrush and juniper, hot springs, green valleys, and pine-covered forests. From the Pendleton Roundup to ghost towns like Granite, the history of the pioneers, the gold seekers, the cowboys and the ranchers is visible all around.

Step in the ruts of the Old Oregon Trail and see live actors interpret life on the trail at the Oregon Trail Interpretive Center at Baker City and at the Oregon Trail Interpretive Park east of Pendleton. The interpretive center at Baker City is a "must see" if you are in the area.

The kids will also enjoy a ride on the old Sumpter Railway at McEwen Station to the old mining town of Sumpter. See magnificent mountains as you ride on the steepest tramway in North America. Feel like an early pioneer as you walk the streets of Pendleton. Try your hand at panning gold in Granite.

If you or the kids are interested in rocks and geology, you will enjoy the three areas of the John Day Fossil Beds National Monument.

As in most of Oregon, parks are plentiful and provide abundant opportunities to picnic, camp, fish, swim, and hike. We listed the ones with special attractions for children, but you may want to try some of the many others.

Enjoy the Old West as you experience Eastern Oregon.

Pictures on preceding page, from upper left clockwise: Covered wagon information center at a scenic view area, Sumpter Valley Train at McEwen Station, John Day Fossil Beds - Painted Hills Section

The Pendleton Area

Pendleton is an interesting town with several exciting things to do. It is the host of the famous annual Pendleton Roundup in September. This world-famous rodeo draws thousands of visitors. Listed below are a few other things that can be fun and interesting in and around Pendleton.

PENDLETON ROUNDUP HALL OF FAME

The Pendleton Roundup Hall of Fame contains a collection of cowboy, rodeo, and Native American memorabilia. Pictures of past and present rodeo champions are prominent, as are pictures of the past and present rodeo queens and princesses. There is a great collection of handsome old saddles. Beautiful examples of Indian beading and costumes of past princesses are also featured. A small park with playground equipment and picnic tables is adjacent to the grounds and will provide a chance for you to relax and for the kids to stretch their legs.

Location: S.W. Court Street, lower level of the South Grandstand of the Pendleton Roundup Stadium, Pendleton (541) 276-2553

✪, RR, GS

LIVING HERITAGE TOURS OF NORTHEAST OREGON

Choose a 1 1/2 hour or a 3 hour tour in a modern day prairie schooner (an air-conditioned van) which takes you to the Umatilla Indian Reservation, the Old Oregon and Walla Walla Trails, the Old West Boom Town of Adams, and through the surrounding agricultural land. Another feature of the tour is to visit and see how an old wood crib grain elevator works and to see other ways that farming has changed in the last one hundred years. Open daily during the summer months from 8:30 a. m. to 6:00 p. m. Reservations are suggested.

Location: 239 S. E. Court, Pendleton. (541)278-2446
$$$

PENDLETON UNDERGROUND TOURS

In Pendleton's Old Town, take an exciting tour of the city's famous underground tunnels. The tour will provide a look at Pendleton's interesting past and explain why the Chinese laborers built this underground city. The tour lasts for 90 minutes and includes a 1920's ice cream party, a Chinese laundry, a meat market, and other businesses. It also includes a bawdy house which visitors may choose to exclude if they wish. The tour guide provides a commentary on the life of the time. The tours are available all year long but check for seasonal hours. Reservations recommended.

Location: 37 S.W. Emigrant, Pendleton, OR (503) 276-0730
$$$

OREGON TRAIL INTERPRETIVE PARK AT BLUE MOUNTAIN CROSSING

This interpretive park contains well-preserved wagon ruts from the Old Oregon Trail. There is a half-mile paved path that leads past ceramic interpretive panels depicting the life on the Oregon Trail. On most weekends during the summer, real life dramatizations portray the pioneer life along the Oregon Trail. The park is open from Memorial Day to Labor Day from 8:00 a.m. to 8:00 p.m.

Location: Off exit 248 on 1-84 east of Pendleton. 1-800-848-9969
✪, RR, PT, DW

THE WALLOWA MOUNTAINS

East of La Grande lie the magnificent Wallowa Mountains and the Eagle Cap Wilderness, sometimes called the "Switzerland of America." This area once was the home of the Nez Perce Indians. A monument near Wallowa Lake in the Wallowa Mountains, honors Chief Joseph, the famous leader of the Nez Perce. The area offers a multitude of recreational opportunities in both winter and summer. Below are two of the many interesting things to visit.

WALLOWA LAKE TRAMWAY

Enjoy a ride in a four passenger gondola, on the steepest tramway in North America. The fifteen minute ride to the top of 8256 foot, Mt. Howard, is breathtaking. You can see into four states, the Eagle Cap Wilderness, and into the blue waters of Wallowa Lake. You will look down on mountain tops which resemble the Swiss Alps. As you ascend the mountain you will be at an average height of 30 feet above the ground. At the top of Mt. Howard there are two miles of hiking trails. There is also a restaurant at the summit. The tramway is open seasonally from late May through September.

Location: On Highway 82 at Wallowa Lake, (541) 432-5331
$$$, RR, R

MANUEL MUSEUM

The Manuel Museum should be interesting to both kids and adults. The museum is dedicated to the history of the Nez Perce Indians.The upstairs section houses an art gallery which features bronze sculptures by David Manuel, the official sculptor of the Oregon Trail. Art by other artists is also exhibited. Art demonstrations take place throughout the day. A huge collection of Native American artifacts and Old West memorabilia is also displayed. In the basement is a children's museum, featuring a miniature tepee encampment and a wagon train, as well as a cafe. The museum is open from 9:00 a.m. to 5:00 p.m. seven days a week. Tour guides are available.

Location: 400 N. Main Street, Joseph, Oregon (541) 432-7235
$, RR, PT, DW, GS

Baker City Area

There are many things to do in and around Baker City. You may wish to stay there as you take time to see some of the things located in Baker City and within a twenty-five mile radius. The Baker County Visitors' Association at 490 Campbell St., Baker City (1-800-523-1235) is very helpful. Besides having many useful brochures and a helpful staff, it has an small but interesting mini-museum housed upstairs. Open daily 8:00- 5:00 during the summer. Monday - Friday 8-5, during the remainder of the year.

JET BOATING AND WHITE-WATER RAFTING ON THE SNAKE RIVER

There are many companies offering different types of boating on the Snake River into the Hells Canyon area. Various types of boating adventures are offered daily from May to September. If you are interested in such a trip, contact the Baker County Visitors' Association.

Location: Baker County Visitors' Association, 490 Campbell, Baker City. 1-800-523-1235.
$$$

OREGON TRAIL INTERPRETIVE CENTER

If you plan to visit any historical sights in Oregon, this is surely a must-see. Allow at least two hours for a visit to this superb center.

The museum contains life-like and life-size permanent

exhibits of life on the Oregon Trail. As you look at the exhibits, you will hear realistic sounds that compliment each exhibit. There are also other permanent and changing displays of pioneer life.

Demonstrations of pioneer arts and skills are presented by costumed volunteers. Stage shows and slide shows are given both at the inside theater and at the outside amphitheater. Outside the museum is an approximately four-mile trail winding around Flagstaff Hill. Along the trail, visitors can see other sights and sounds of the Oregon Trail. Visitors of all ages will find something of interest in this wonderful interpretive center. Open Daily at 9.

Location: West of Baker City on Flagstaff Hill, five miles east of junction I-84 and SR 86, (541) 523-1843

○, RR, PT, DW, GS

OREGON TRAIL REGIONAL MUSEUM

The Oregon Trail Regional Museum is a large and important museum. It houses a large collection of rocks and minerals which is one of the best in the United States. Pioneer, mining, Native American, farming, and ranching exhibits are also featured. A horse-drawn trolley ride through Baker can be taken from the museum. There is a fee for this ride. Geiser Pollman Park is across the street from the museum. See following page.

Location: 2480 Grove, Baker City. (1-800-523-1235)

$, RR, DW, GS

GEISER POLLMAN PARK

Across the street from the Oregon Trail Regional Museum is a city park where the kids can run, or play on the playground equipment. Picnic tables are plentiful and the many trees make the park cool and inviting. You can spend some relaxing time in this pleasant city park.

Location: Across the street from the Oregon Trail Regional Museum in Baker City.

✪, RR,PT, DW

SUMPTER VALLEY RAILWAY

Only 24 miles southwest of Baker City, is McEwen train station. Board an old-fashioned wood burning train which will take you on a five-mile round-trip ride to the old gold mining town of Sumpter. The length of the ride is just right and the whole family will enjoy a ride on a train of yesterday. In Sumpter you can walk around the little western town and see old dredging equipment which the gold miners once used. While waiting to board the train at the McEwen Station, have a picnic and try to spot the wildlife at the adjacent Oregon Wildlife Game Habitat Preserve. There is also playground equipment available. The train runs all day on Saturday, Sundays, and holidays from Memorial Day weekend through the last weekend in September.

Location: 24 miles SW of Baker City on Highway 7 (541-894-2268)

$$, RR, PT

GRANITE GHOST TOWN

Out of Sumpter, a winding road takes you fifteen miles to the ghost town of Granite. A few people still live in Granite, but there are empty buildings which remind you of its gold-mining past. In the summer months, visitors may pan for gold in the nearby creek. In the area around Granite there are camping, hiking, fishing, and berry-picking opportunities. Snowmobile rides and cross country skiing are possible in the winter months.

Location: Highway 7
✪, R, GS

EASTERN OREGON MUSEUM

This museum houses a large collection of antique toys, including many dolls. It also has a reconstructed blacksmith shop, kitchen, parlor, old saloon, and a late 1800s train depot. There are also many farming and mining artifacts. Open April 15 - October 15 from 9:00 - 5:00. By appointment during the rest of the year.

Location: 3rd & School, Haines (541) 856-3233
✪, RR

JOHN DAY FOSSIL BEDS NATIONAL MONUMENT

Enjoy the geological wonders in this interesting area of the state. The fossil beds here contain a fascinating record of ancient life. There are fossils of bones, leaves, nuts, seeds, and wood. The John Day Fossil Beds contain some of the richest fossil beds in the world. This national monument is divided into three sections: the Clarno Unit, the Painted Hills Unit, and the Sheep Rock Unit. The Clarno Unit has cliffs formed by ancient mud flows which covered a forested area, leaving the fossilized remains. The Painted Hills Unit is breathtaking with its soft rolling hills of red, pink, bronze, tan, and black. These clay stone hills were formed by the weathering of volcanic ash. The Sheep Rock Unit contains most of the fossil beds to be found in the area. The information headquarters is located in the town of John Day at 420 West Main Street. All the units offer beautiful and interesting geographical landscapes and well-kept hiking trails. A park ranger is usually available to answer questions and there are informative displays. If you plan to spend several hours in visiting one or all three of these spectacular areas, take a picnic lunch and don't forget your camera!

Location: The Clarno Unit: 18 miles west of Fossil, OR along SR 218

The Painted Hills Unit: 9 miles northwest of Mitchell, OR, off US 26

The Sheep Rock Unit: 6 miles north of Dayville, at the intersection of US 26 and SR 19. (541) 987-2333

✪, RR, PT, DW, I

Notes

Chapter 6

Explore Southern Oregon

6

Introduction

Southern Oregon has many places to see, from the spectacular and unique Crater Lake National Park to the bizarre phenomena at the House of Mystery at the Oregon Vortex. The Siskiyou Mountains cross the area from north to south with Interstate 5 providing a fast and easy way to travel in the area. There are fruit producing valleys such as those around Medford, but also many forests. The southeastern area has rugged terrain but great beauty as evidenced in the Steen Mountain area. The Oregon Caves are awe-inspiring and the historic town of Jacksonville both interesting and amusing.

Museums are abundant with the Pacific Northwest Museum of Natural History at Ashland, and the Children's Museum at Jacksonville especially appealing to children.

Wildlife Safari, a drive-through park where wild animals are roaming free, is sure to be of interest to children. Jet boat rides on the Rogue River and seeing how dogs are trained to be hearing ear dogs are other attractions sure to please the kids.

With the beauty of plentiful forests and fruitful valleys, and interesting places to visit from both the historic past and the exciting present, there are sure to be things for both you and the kids to enjoy in Southern Oregon.

Pictures on preceding page, clock-wise from upper left: Viewing animals at Wildlife Safari from car window, fishing at pond, Crater Lake National Park

Ashland and Medford Area

DOGS FOR THE DEAF

Most kids love dogs, so they will probably enjoy visiting Dogs for the Deaf, a center where dogs are trained to help the deaf by responding to normal household sounds. The trained dogs are then placed nationwide with persons needing this type of assistance. The dogs used in the training are usually rescued from pounds. Visitors may tour the facility and see a demonstration of one of the dogs actually in training. Tours are held from May through September, Monday-Saturday, hourly from 10 -2. During the other months the facility is open, but tours are not held as often. Phone for times.

Location: 10175 Wheeler Road, just off I-5 near Central Point and Medford (541) 826-9220

✪, RR, DW, GS

EMIGRANT LAKE

Six miles south of Ashland is Emigrant Lake, a popular recreation area. Fishing, boating, swimming, waterskiing, sailing, and windsurfing are all popular activities on the lake. Other activities are picnicking, volleyball, and horseshoe pits. Sure to please the kids is a splash pool with a large water slide.

Open from Memorial Day - Labor Day.

Location: Take exit 14 off I-5 near Ashland, east on Highway 66, watch for signs. (541) 776-7001

$ (Extra fee for splash pool), RR, PT, DW, SB

JACKSONVILLE (NATIONAL HISTORIC MONUMENT)

For a step-back in time, visit historic Jacksonville, an old gold-mining town. There are walking tours of the 80 still-standing buildings from the early 1850s, or in the summer you may take a horse-drawn ride through the quaint old town. There are also trolley ride tours. Visitors can see a working gold mine and pan for gold. There is a large museum which you may visit which has well-produced life-sized exhibits. Jacksonville is not a ghost town, but rather a town with a well-preserved past.

Location: Exit 32 from I-5 Chamber of Commerce: (541) 899-8118

◎ (to walk around the town yourself—tours, shops, museums etc. for a fee), RR, DW, I, SB, R, GS

JACKSONVILLE CHILDREN'S MUSEUM

This "hands-on" children's museum offers children a look-back in time with its many replicas of buildings and places of yesterday. In the museum, which was formerly a 1910 jailhouse, children can experience life as it used to be in replicas of an old school, store, barbershop, bank, etc. There is also an extensive collection of old toys. Adjacent to the children's museum is the Jacksonville Museum of Southern Oregon History which might be of interest to older children. Open Memorial Day through Labor Day from 10:00 - 5:00. Remainder of the year Tuesday - Sunday with shortened hours. Closed New Year's Day, Thanksgiving, and Christmas.

Location: 206 North 5th Street, Jacksonville (541) 773-6536

$ (under 6 free), RR, PT, DW, I, GS

LITHIA PARK

If you are in Ashland, spend a little time in beautiful Lithia Park. Located next to the famous Oregon

Shakespeare Theater, this 99 acre park boasts spring water which comes through pipes from a spring which bubbles up in the Cascade foothills. The park which borders on Ashland Creek, also has hiking and nature trails, a large playground, Japanese gardens, and picnic areas. Bring a picnic and relax for an hour or two in Lithia Park.

Location: Ashland, OR
✪, RR, PT, DW

OREGON SHAKESPEARE THEATRE

Located in the attractive town of Ashland, the world-famous Oregon Shakespeare Theater offers indoor and outdoor plays from mid-February through October 31st. While plays by Shakespeare are the primary focus, there are other plays also produced. Some kids will enjoy seeing a play by Shakespeare because of the action involved and the extravagant costumes. Backstage tours will interest most ages. A visit to the Fantasy Gallery will let children try on costumes, pose for pictures, and walk on the stage. There are also other theaters in Ashland, so check with the Chamber of Commerce if you think your children would be interested. (541) 482-3486.

Location: 15 South Pioneer Street, Ashland. (541) 482-4331
$$$, RR, DW, SB, GS

PACIFIC NORTHWEST MUSEUM OF NATURAL HISTORY

The kids are sure to have fun and enjoy learning about natural history in this new interpretive center for the entire family. There are multi-sensory exhibits, interactive computer adventures, hands-on games, and live animal shows. Kids (and adults) can try some science experiments in the hands-on Discovery Lab or take a walk

within the magma walls of a volcanic lava tube. Open daily during the summer from 9:00 - 5:00, Remainder of the year: Wednesday - Friday 10:00 - 4:00, Saturday - Sunday 10:00 - 5:00

Location: 1500 East Main Street, Ashland 1-800-637-8581 or (541) 488-1084
$$ (under 3 - free), RR, PT, DW, GS

Klamath Falls Area

COLLIER MEMORIAL STATE PARK

If you think the kids would enjoy a picnic in a park which boasts a pioneer village and an antique logging exhibit, then make a stop at Collier Memorial State Park. The pioneer village contains a doctor's office, a store, outhouses, and a smokehouse as well as homes of early pioneers. The homes reveal differing styles of construction from the primitive explorer's cabin with its dirt floor and fire pit, to a more comfortable home with glass windows, a wood floor, and a cast iron stove. There are plentiful examples of early logging equipment, picnic areas, and a nature trail which follows the river and creek. The park is either for camping or day use.

Location: U.S. 97, 30 miles north of Klamath Falls. (541) 783-2471
$ (day use fee), RR, PT, DW, I, GS (Information booth and gift shop open summers only.)

FAVELL MUSEUM OF WESTERN ART AND INDIAN ARTIFACTS

Favell Museum is a large museum, dedicated to the Indians of the area. Its theme is "Reflecting the Heritage of the West." Kids might be most interested in the extensive arrowhead collection or in the large collection of miniature firearms. There are many beautiful exhibits of Indian art, including stonework, quill work, pottery, basketry, beadwork, and carvings. A gallery of western art is also housed in this museum. Open Monday through Saturday from 9:30 - 5:30. Closed on Sundays

Location: 125 West Main St., Klamath Falls, (541) 882-9996
$ (under age 6 - Free) RR, DW, GS

ST. JOHN'S MINIATURE RAILROAD
Operated by the Over-the-Hill Live Steam Club, this miniature train has cars large enough for adults and runs on a mile and a half loop. On the loop is a miniature old west village called Mercedes. The engineer will stop the train at the village and tell about it. Open from the middle of June until Labor Day. Call for hours.

Location: 36951 South Chiloquin Rd. in Chiloquin (541) 783-2554
$, RR, PT, DW

Lakeview Area
OLD PERPETUAL GEYSER
Old Perpetual Geyser spouts sixty feet in the air at approximately 90 second intervals. Though located at the Hunter's Hot Springs Resort, you need not be a guest to view this geyser, Oregon's answer to Old Faithful. You may picnic near the geyser or feed the ducks in the pond. There is a charge to use the mineral pool, fed by hot springs, or the other facilities at Hunter's Hot Springs. Open year round.

Location: Highway 395, 1 mile north of Lakeview. (541) 947-4800.
✪, PT (RR, I, SB, R, GS located in Hunter's Hot Springs Resort)

SCHMINCK MEMORIAL MUSEUM

Clothes of the past are a special feature of this museum. There are also old dolls and school lunch boxes of long ago. Arrowheads and other Indian artifacts are on display. Some of the exhibits in the museum are of the "hands-on" type. There is a park with restrooms and picnic facilities two blocks away and a restaurant across the street. The museum is open from 1-5 on Tuesday - Saturday. Closed during December, January and major holidays.

Location: 1 block off of U.S. 395 at 128 S.E. Street. (541) 947-3134
$, I

Other Southern Oregon Attractions

CRATER LAKE NATIONAL PARK

Crater Lake National Park, Oregon's only national park, is also one of the loveliest in the United States. It is the sixth oldest national park. Crater Lake was formed when Mt. Mazama erupted nearly 7,000 years ago. This lake's famous deep blue color results from the crystal clear water and the exceptional depth, 1,932 feet. It is the deepest lake in the United States and the seventh deepest in the world. Rim Drive, a 33 mile drive, encircles the lake and passes Vidae Falls with many overlooks along the way. This drive is only open from mid-July to mid-October. In the center of the lake is beautiful Wizard Island, rising 760 feet above the lake's surface. During the summer you can experience the lake and its beauty by taking a guided boat tour around the lake. Two-hour boat trips are regularly scheduled from July through September. Guides explain the geological and ecological features of the area as the boat cruises the 25-mile perimeter of the lake. If you prefer hiking to cruising there are more than 90 miles of maintained trails. Even the youngest children will enjoy walking through wildflower-covered meadows. Park rangers provide special programs for children as well as guided hikes. Though busiest during the summer, there are also things to do during the winter, such as cross-country skiing. There are lodging and camping facilities within the park. During summer months you may learn about Crater Lake at the Steel Information Center at Park Headquarters or at Rim Village Visitor Centers. From October through early June, Rim Drive and the park's north entrance are closed due to snow . Winter access is only available to Rim Village on Highway 62. All-weather roads are open to Steel Information Center from the south and west park entrances. Visitor Center open 9-5, closed December 25.

Location: Crater Lake Highway 62 (541) 594-2511
$ (National Park entrance fee per car), RR, PT, DW, I, SB, R, GS

HOUSE OF MYSTERY AND THE OREGON VORTEX

The Oregon Vortex area has been known for many years. The early Indians called it "The Forbidden Ground" and stayed away from it. The circular area known as the Oregon Vortex is a field of force, half above and half below the ground. A guide will explain and demonstrate the phenomena that occurs there. The House of Mystery exhibits examples of the phenomena as does the surrounding area. Some of the strange things that happen are: as a person goes away from you towards the south he/she appears taller, when he approaches he/she becomes shorter. This is the opposite of the laws of perspective and has to be seen to be believed. Nowhere in the circle of the Vortex can you stand erect. You will inevitably incline toward the magnetic north. The trees in the circle also incline toward the magnetic north. Models and displays are available to help you understand what you are seeing. While pictures are available for purchase, you are invited to bring your own still camera to photograph the strange world of the House of Mystery and the Oregon Vortex. Older children will enjoy trying to figure out the scientific reasons for the strange things that happen here. Younger children will be surprised at the strange phenomena. Open March through October. Hours: June, July, August - 9:00 - 6:00 (last tour at 5:15) March, April, May, Sept, October 15: 9:00 a. m. - 5:00 (Last Tour at 4:15)

Location:430 Sardine Creek Road, Gold Hill, (541) 855-1543
$$, RR, GS

OREGON CAVES NATIONAL MONUMENT

Called the "Marble Halls of Oregon", the Oregon Caves National Monument is located in the Siskiyou Mountains. The marble in the caves was formed millions of years ago from seashells under an ocean. The seashells recrystallized to form limestone. Later the limestone was recrystallized to become marble. The caves have about 3 miles of passages and rooms. The largest room, the Ghost Room, is 240 feet long, 50 feet wide, and 40 feet high. The caves are called living caves because stalactites and stalagmites are still being formed. Many kinds of bats inhabit the caves, with the Townsend's Big-eared Bat being the most commonly seen. There are also pack-rats, cave crickets, and giant Pacific salamanders living in the caves. Tour guides accompany visitors and offer informative and interesting insights on the caves. The average temperature of the caves is 41 degrees so dress warmly if you tour them. Wear comfortable shoes because you will be climbing and the floor of the cave is often wet. Children under six are not allowed in the caves and it is also recommended that people with heart, circulation, or breathing difficulties not take the cave tour. If you are able to take the tour, you and the children will find it awe-inspiring. There are hiking trails around the cave and located close by is the historic Oregon Caves Chateau which has lodging, a restaurant, and gift shop. Open daily 8-7 mid-June through Labor Day, 9-5 for the remainder of the year. Closed Thanksgiving and Christmas.

Location: From Cave Junction, 20 miles east on State Road 46. (541) 592-3400
$$, RR, R, GS

BOATING ON THE ROGUE RIVER

From Grants Pass, Gold Beach, or Agness, you can take an exciting trip on the Rogue River. Trips are scheduled on jet boats, white water rafts, or kayaks. A favorite trip is a jet boat ride on the Rogue. Most trips are narrated by seasoned guides who entertain as well as inform you. The guide will point out the wildlife and the natural and man-made scenery. You may expect to see deer, beaver, osprey, blue herons, and even an occasional bear. The gorgeous scenery the river passes through is spectacular and none more so than the steep walls of Hellgate Canyon. Kayak, whitewater rafts, and drift boats are also available for trips on the river, which has been designated by Congress as a "Wild and Scenic River". Part of the area through which the river trips take is a wilderness area which is protected from the encroachments of civilization. Check out which trips are best for the ages of your own children. There are many businesses in the area who provide trips of varying difficulty and duration.

Location: Check with Grants Pass Visitor and Convention Bureau 1-800-547-5927
$$$

WILDLIFE SAFARI

Plan to spend an entire day at the Wildlife Safari. This is Oregon's only drive-through game park and will give  you and the kids an excellent opportunity to see wild animals in a free environment. With the price of admission, you may drive through the park twice. In this 600 acre reserve you may expect to see bears, cheetahs, elephants, emus, lions, hippos, and rhinos among other animals. After your driving tour of the park you may visit the village where there are restaurants, snack bars, and gift shops. There is also a petting zoo and an Education Center. You may ride on a train or ride on an elephant. There are also a wide variety of animal shows, films, and exhibits. If you prefer picnicking to restaurants, there is an area where you may bring your own picnic. If you are traveling with pets, there are free kennels available. Open daily year-round, 9 a.m. in the fall, winter, and spring, 8:30 a.m. in summer. Closing hours vary from 4 p.m. in the winter to 8 p.m. in the summer. Call ahead for current hours.

Location: Take Exit 119 from I-5 (6 miles south of Roseburg). Follow Hwy. 42 towards Winston. Turn right on Lookingglass Rd., then right on Safari Rd. (180 miles south of Portland) (541) 679-6761

$$$, RR, PT, DW, R, SB, GS

Notes

Notes

Index

Place Names and Page Numbers

A

A. R. Bowman Museum (Prineville) 88
Alpenrose Dairy (Portland) 54
Amazon Park (Eugene) 39
American Advertising Museum 54
Astoria Column (Astoria) 4
Aurora Colony Museum (Aurora) 47

B

Bandon Cheese 33
Bastendorff County Park (North Bend) 29
Beverly Cleary Sculpture Garden (Portland) 54
Boating on the Rogue River (Gold Beach, Grants Pass, Agness) 113
Boating on the Umpqua (Reedsport) 26
Bonneville Dam and Fish Hatchery (Columbia River Gorge) 67
Blue Heron Cheese Factory (Tillamook) 9
Bumper Cars and Arcade (Seaside) 7

C

C & M Stables (Florence Area) 23
Cape Kiwanda (Pacific City) 12
Cape Meares Lighthouse (Tillamook Area) 10
Cape Perpetua Visitor's Center (Waldport - Yachats Area) 21
Carnegie Center Children's Museum 65
Cascade Sternwheelers (Portland) 55
Champoeg State Park (St. Paul Area) 48
Children's Museum (Portland) 55
Children's Nature Museum (Seaside) 7
Clackamas Country Historical Society Museum (Oregon City) 65
Coast Guard Air Station (North Bend Air Station) 28
Coast Guard Cutter Orcas (Coos Bay) 32
Collier Memorial State Park (Klamath Falls) 108
Columbia River Maritime Museum (Astoria) 4
Coos Bay Downtown Boardwalk 31
Cove Palisades State Park (Madras Area) 89
Crater Lake (Southern Oregon) 110

D

D River State Wayside (Lincoln City) 14
Darlingtonia Wayside (Florence Area) 23
Dean Creek Elk Viewing Area (Reedsport Area) 27
Depoe Bay 15
Deschutes Historical Center (Bend) 78
Detroit Lake Recreation Area (Off Highway 22) 47
Devil's Elbow State Park (Florence Area) 22
Devil's Punch Bowl State Park (Highway 101 - Depoe Bay Area) 15
Dogs for the Deaf (Ashland) 105
Dollywares Doll Museum (Florence) 24
Drake Park (Bend) 78

E

Eastern Oregon Museum (Haines) 101
Emigrant Lake (Ashland) 105
Empire Lakes Park (North Bend) 29
Enchanted Forest (Salem Area) 41
End of the Oregon Trail Interpretive Center (Oregon City) 66

F

Favell Museum (Klamath Falls) 108
Flower Gardens in the Willamette Valley 44
Flying M Ranch (McMinnville Area) 46
Fogarty Creek State Park (Highway 101 near Depot Bay) 14
Fort Clatsop (Astoria Area) 5
Fort Stevens (Astoria Area) 6
Funny Farm (Bend Area) 78

G

Geiser Pollman Park (Baker City) 100
Gilbert House Children's Museum (Salem) 43
Granite Ghost Town 100

H

Hart's Reptile World 48
Hatfield Marine Science Center (Newport) 18
Headwaters of the Metolius (Sisters Area) 87
The Hero (Reedsport) 27
High Desert Museum (Bend Area) 79
Historic Alsea Bridge Interpretive Center (Waldport) 20
Honeyman State Park (Florence Area) 25
House of Mystery and Oregon Vortex (Gold Hill Area) 111

I

Ice Skating Rinks (Bend Area) 80

J

Jacksonville 106
Jacksonville Children's Museum 106
Jeff Morris Fire Museum (Portland) 56
Jet Boating (Gold Beach) 33
Jet Boating and White Water Rafting - Snake River (Baker City) 98
John Day Fossil Beds National Monuments (Near John Day) 101
John Inskeep Environmental Learning Center (Oregon City) 67

K

Kid Zone and Museum (Redmond) 85
Kidd's Toy Museum (Portland) 56

L

Lane County Ice Rink (Eugene) 39
Latimer Quilt Center (Tillamook) 10
Lava Cast Forest (Bend Area) 80
Lava Butte and Lavalands Visitor Center (Bend Area) 80
Lava River Cave (Bend Area) 81
Lithia Park (Ashland) 106
Living Heritage Tours of Northeast Oregon (Pendleton) 95
Lloyd Center (Portland) 57
Loeb State Park (Gold Beach Area) 34
Lookout Creek Old Growth Trail (Eugene Area) 39

M

Manuel Museum (Joseph) 97
Marshfield Sun (Coos Bay)   31
Menasha Timber Corporation Woods Tour (Coos Bay) 32
Metro Washington Park (Portland) 57
Metro Washington Park Zoo (Portland) 58
Mike Miller Educational Area (Newport Area) 20
Mingus Park (Coos Bay) 32
Mission Mill Village (Salem) 43
Mollala Miniature Steam Trains (Mollala) 49
Mount Bachelor (Bend Area) 81
Mount Hood Meadows and Multipor (Mount Hood) 72
Mount Hood Scenic Railroad (Hood River) 69
Mount Hood SkiBowl (Mount Hood)   72
Multnomah Falls (Columbia Gorge - off I-84) 70

Museum at Warm Springs   90
Museum of Natural History (Eugene) 40

N
Newberry National Volcanic Monument (Bend Area) 82
Nike Town (Portland) 59
North Clackamas Aquatic Park (Portland) 59

O
Oaks Park (Portland) 59
Old Perpetual Geyser (Lakeview) 109
Operation Santa Claus (Redmond Area) 85
Oregon Candy Farm (Highway 26 on way to Mount Hood 71
Oregon Caves (Southern Oregon) 112
Oregon City Municipal Elevator 64
Oregon Coast Aquarium (Newport) 18
Oregon Dunes National Recreation Area (Florence Area) 26
Oregon History Center (Portland) 60
Oregon Maritime Center and Museum (Portland 61
Oregon Museum of Science & Industry - OMSI (Portland) 61
Oregon Shakespeare Theater (Ashland) 107
Oregon State Capitol Building 44
Oregon Trail Interpretive Center at Baker City 98
Oregon Trail Interpretive Park at Blue Mtn Crossing (Pendleton Area) 96
Oregon Trail Regional Museum (Baker City) 99

P
Pacific Northwest Museum of Natural History (Ashland) 107
Paul Jensen Arctic Museum (Monmouth) 46
Pendleton Roundup Hall of Fame 95
Pendleton Underground Tours 96
Petersen Rock Gardens (Redmond Area) 86
Phoenix & Holly Railroad - The Flower Farm (Canby) 49
Pine Mountain Observatory (Highway 20 East of Bend) 89
Portland Police Museum 62
Prehistoric Gardens (Port Orford Area) 34

R
Rainbow Trout Fishing Farm (Near Sandy) 73
Regatta Grounds Park (Lincoln City) 13
Ripley's Believe It or Not (Newport) 19
Road's End State Wayside (Lincoln City Area) 13

S

St. John's Miniature Railroad (Chiloquin Area) 109
Salt Works (Seaside) 8
SAMTRAK (Portland) 63
Sand Biking 8
Sand Dunes Frontier and Theme Park (Florence) 25
Sandland Adventures (Florence) 24
Saragosa Old West Recreation Park (Eugene Area) 40
Saturday Market (Eugene Area) 40
Saturday Market (Portland Area) 62
Schmink Museum (Lakeview) 110
Sea Lion Caves (Florence Area) 22
Seaside Aquarium 8
Shaniko Ghost Town (Bend Area) 90
Shevlin Park (Bend) 82
Shore Acres Botanical Gardens State Park 30
Silver Falls State Park (Salem Area) 45
Smith Rocks State Park (Redmond Area) 86
SPLASH! The Lively Park Swim Center (Eugene Area) 41
Sternwheeler Columbia Gorge (Cascade Locks) 70
Sumpter Valley Railway 100
Sunriver (Bend Area) 83
Sunriver Nature Center (Bend Area) 83
Sunset Bay State Park (North Bend Area) 30
Sweetbriar Park 42

T

The Dalles 68
The Dalles Dam and Tour Train Ride 69
Tenmile Lakes County Park 29
Thrillville USA (Salem Area) 42
Tillamook Cheese Factory 11
Tillamook County Pioneer Museum 11
Tillamook Naval Air Museum 12
Timberline (Mount Hood) 73
Town Center Carousel 9
Trail of Dreams Sled Dog Rides (Bend Area) 84
Tryon Creek State Park (Portland) 63

U

Umpqua Discovery Center (Reedsport) 26
Umpqua River Lighthouse State Park 28
Undersea Gardens (Newport) 19
U.S. Coast Guard Station (Newport) 17
Uppertown Firefighter's Museum (Astoria) 6

W

Wallowa Mountains (Joseph Area) 97
Wallowa Lake Tramway (Joseph Area) 97
Waxworks - A Living Museum (Newport) 19
West Coast Game Park Safari (Bandon Area) 33
Wet Willie's Bumper Boats (Bend) 84
White Water Raft Trips (Bend Area) 84
Wildlife Safari (Roseburg Area - Winston) 114
WISTEC Children's Museum (Eugene Area) 41
Wizard Falls Fish Hatchery (Off Highway 20) 88
Wonder Works Children's Museum (The Dalles) 68
World Forestry Center (Portland) 63

Y

Yachats Commons Playground 20
Yaquina Bay State Park (Newport) 17
Yaquina Head   (Newport Area)16

ADDENDUM - 1997

CHANGES: Most state and federal parks listed as free or small donation for day use, now charge a small fee.

DELETIONS: The Discovery Zones listed for Lloyd Center and Beaverton (Page 57) are no longer operating. Saragosa Park (page 40) is no longer in operation.

ADDITIONS: The Columbia Gorge Discovery Center is now open in The Dalles. The Wasco County Historical Museum, adjacent to the Center is also open. Informative videos are found throughout the center. Special events are scheduled periodically. With both indoor and outdoor displays, there should be something for most ages to enjoy. Open: 10-6 daily, closed New Year's Day, Thanksgiving, and Christmas

Location: 5000 Discovery Drive, The Dalles, OR 97058, Take exit 82 from I-84.   (541) 296-8600

$$ (children under 5 free), RR, PT, DW, R, I, GS
- -
The Four Rivers Cultural Center opened May 31, 1997. The center features a museum and a theater. It highlights the people and culture of the Paiutes, the Japanese, Basques, Hispanic, and others who have influenced the area around Ontario, Oregon. You can discover their customs and costumes at the center. One area will be especially interesting for children. There will be hands-on activities and special programs to interest kids. Open daily from 9-5, closed Thanksgiving, Christmas, and New Year's Day.

Location: 676 SW 5th Ave. Ontario ,OR. Take I-84 to Exit 376.   (888) 211-1222

$$ (under 5 free), RR, DW, R (open in fall of '97), GS

ADDENDUM - 1998

CHANGES: Telephone # for Splash Swim Center- Page 41, has been changed to: (541)726-2752.
Yaquina Head Lighthouse (Page 16) Tel. # is now: (541) 574-3100

DELETIONS: Pacific NW Museum of Natural History in Ashland, (Page 107) is now closed. They hope to reopen at some time in the future.

ADDITIONS: Yaquina Head Interpretive Center opened in 1998. The theme of this center is "Partners in Protection" (teaching responsible use of the Oregon Coast). It is part of the Yaquina Head Lighthouse area which includes 100 acres of tide pools and nature trails. Exhibits are interesting to all ages and include hands on activities and an introductory video.
Location: Off Hwy 101 between Newport & Waldport   (541) 574-3100
$ (children under 5 free), RR, DW, I, GS

University of Oregon Museum of Natural History in Eugene has many archeological, anthropological and natural science exhibits. Several hands-on activities make this fun for all ages.
Location: 1680 E. 15th, Eugene, OR. (541) 346-3024
✪ RR, DW, GS

Recreation Station in McMinnville. This large play structure located in the city park is fun for many ages of kids. It features climbing, crawling, swinging, and discovery activities. Plenty of room here for parents to sit on benches to wait for the kids and watch them having fun.
Location: City Park off Highway 99.
✪ RR, DW, PT

A. C. Gilbert Discovery Village is opening in June of 1998.   It has miniature village, musical ensemble deck, interactive activities, giant erector set, weather station, a discovery garden, a woolly mammoth dig, and an amphitheater. Take a ride on a large model of the American Flyer Train. It is a new part of the Gilbert House Children's Museum.
Location: 116 Marion St. NE, Salem. (503)371-3631
$$, RR, DW, PT, GS

Fir Point Farm near Aurora has a nature trail, White Rabbit Hole, small animals to pet, along with a nursery and farm produce. There are special seasonal activities for children.
Location: 14600 Arndt Road, Aurora (503) 678-2455
✪ RR, SB, GS

State of Oregon Sports Hall of Fame contains interactive exhibits, traveling exhibits, and sports memorabilia. Open Tues-Sun. 10-6
Location: 321 SW Salmon, Portland   (503) 227-7466
✪ RR, DW, GS

Rose Garden Children's Park has more than 50 activities to delight the kids.   Built so that handicapped children can also enjoy playing there.
Location: Located in the Metro Washington Park near the International Rose Test Gardens. Portland (503)823-2223
✪ RR, PT

Family Fun Center has six acres with batting cages, go-carts, bumper boats, miniature golf, kidopolis, and laser tag. Sun-Th. 11-9, F.-S. 9-11
Location: 29111 SW Town Center Loop, Wilsonville (503) 685-5000
$$ - $$$ (depending on choices) RR, R

Eagle Crest 18-hole Putting course is a challenging putting course complete with water and sand hazards. Fun for any age. Balls and clubs are furnished. Allow 2 hours. Open daily.
Location: 1525 Cline Falls Road. Redmond (541)923-5002
$$, RR, SB, GS

Children's Museum of Eastern Oregon has a toddler exploration room, air and space exhibit, bubble table, shadow room and many more exciting hands-on activities. Open 10-5. Sunday - 1-4
Location: 400 S. Main, Pendleton. (541) 276-1066
$, RR, DW, GS

Wildlife Images Rehabilitation and Education Center gives the visitor a chance to observe the rehabilitation of injured wildlife. Reservations are necessary for this 1 1/2 hour tour and are scheduled twice a day.
Location: 11845 Lower River Road, Grants Pass. (541) 476-0222
✪ (Donation) RR, GS
